MW00756286

The Book of
FORGIVING

Also by Desmond Tutu

God Is Not a Christian

Made for Goodness

Tutu: Authorized

An African Prayer Book

God Has a Dream

No Future Without Forgiveness

The Rainbow People of God

Crying in the Wilderness

Hope and Suffering

The Book of
FORGIVING

The FOURFOLD PATH *for* HEALING
OURSELVES *and* OUR WORLD

DESMOND M. TUTU
and MPHO A. TUTU
Edited by Douglas C. Abrams

HarperOne
An Imprint of HarperCollins*Publishers*

HarperOne

Certain names have been changed where indicated in the text in order to protect the privacy of those individuals.

THE BOOK OF FORGIVING: *The Fourfold Path for Healing Ourselves and Our World.* Copyright © 2014 by Desmond M. Tutu and Mpho A. Tutu. All rights reserved. Printed in the United States of America. No part of this book may be used or reproduced in any manner whatsoever without written permission except in the case of brief quotations embodied in critical articles and reviews. For information address HarperCollins Publishers, 195 Broadway, New York, NY 10007.

HarperCollins books may be purchased for educational, business, or sales promotional use. For information please e-mail the Special Markets Department at SPsales@harpercollins.com.

HarperCollins website: http://www.harpercollins.com

HarperCollins®, 📖®, and HarperOne™ are trademarks of HarperCollins Publishers.

FIRST EDITION

Designed by Matthew Van Zomeren

Library of Congress Cataloging-in-Publication Data

Tutu, Desmond.

The book of forgiving : the fourfold path for healing ourselves and our world / Desmond M. Tutu and Mpho A. Tutu ; edited by Douglas C. Abrams. — FIRST EDITION.

  pages cm

Includes bibliographical references.

ISBN 978-0-06-220356-4

1. Forgiveness. I. Abrams, Douglas Carlton, editor of compilation. II. Title.

BJ1476.T88 2014

179'.9—dc23   2013033890

        18 RRD(H) 10 9

To Angela
We miss you

Contents

Introduction
Into Wholeness

"HE HAD MANY WOUNDS." She spoke with the precision of a coroner. "In the upper abdomen were five wounds. These wounds indicated that different weapons were used to stab him, or a group of people stabbed him." Mrs. Mhlawuli continued her harrowing testimony to the Truth and Reconciliation Commission. She spoke about the disappearance and murder of her husband, Sicelo. "In the lower part, he also had wounds. In total, there were forty-three. They poured acid on his face. They chopped off his right hand just below the wrist. I don't know what they did with that hand." A wave of horror and nausea rose in me.

Now it was nineteen-year-old Babalwa's turn to speak. She was eight when her father died. Her brother was only three. She described the grief, police harassment, and hardship in the years since her father's death. And then she said,

"I would love to know who killed my father. So would my brother." Her next words stunned me and left me breathless. "We want to forgive them. We want to forgive, but we don't know who to forgive."

As chairman of the Truth and Reconciliation Commission, I have often been asked how the people of South Africa were able to forgive the atrocities and injustices they suffered under apartheid. Our journey in South Africa was quite long and treacherous. Today it is hard to believe that, up until our first democratic election in 1994, ours was a country that institutionalized racism, inequality, and oppression. In apartheid South Africa only white people could vote, earn a high-quality education, and expect advancement or opportunity. There were decades of protest and violence. Much blood was shed during our long march to freedom. When, at last, our leaders were released from prison, it was feared that our transition to democracy would become a bloodbath of revenge and retaliation. Miraculously we chose another future. We chose forgiveness. At the time, we knew that telling the truth and healing our history was the only way to save our country from certain destruction. We did not know where this choice would lead us. The process we embarked on through the TRC was, as all real growth proves to be, astoundingly painful and profoundly beautiful.

I have also been asked what I learned about forgiveness from that experience and from the many places I have visited during my life where there has been conflict and suffering, from Northern Ireland to Rwanda. This book is a response to this question. It is also an answer to the unspoken question that lies behind: How *do* we forgive? This book is written for those who need forgiveness, whether they want to forgive or to be forgiven.

There are days when I wish I could erase from my mind all the horrors I have witnessed. It seems there is no end to the creative ways we humans can find to hurt each other, and no end to the reasons we feel justified in doing so. There is also no end to the human capacity for healing. In each of us, there is an innate ability to create joy out of suffering, to find hope in the most hopeless of situations, and to heal any relationship in need of healing.

I would like to share with you two simple truths: there is nothing that cannot be forgiven, and there is no one undeserving of forgiveness. When you can see and understand that we are all bound to one another—whether by birth, by circumstance, or simply by our shared humanity—then you will know this to be true. I have often said that in South Africa there would have been no future without forgiveness. Our rage and our quest for revenge would have been our destruction. This is as true for us individually as it is for us globally.

There have been times when each and every one of us has needed to forgive. There have also been times when each and every one of us has needed to be forgiven. And there will be many times again. In our own ways, we are all broken. Out of that brokenness, we hurt others. Forgiveness is the journey we take toward healing the broken parts. It is how we become whole again.

Whether it is the tormentor who tortured me brutally, the spouse who betrayed me, the boss who passed me over for a promotion, or the driver who cut me off during my morning commute, I face the same choice: to forgive or to seek revenge. We face this choice of whether or not to forgive as individuals, as families, as communities, and as a deeply connected world.

The quality of human life on our planet is nothing more than the sum total of our daily interactions with one another. Each time we help, and each time we harm, we have a dramatic impact on our world. Because we are human, some of our interactions will go wrong, and then we will hurt or be hurt, or both. It is the nature of being human, and it is unavoidable. Forgiveness is the way we set those interactions right. It is the way we mend tears in the social fabric. It is the way we stop our human community from unraveling.

There are countless studies that enumerate the social, spiritual, psychological, and even physiological benefits of forgiveness. The actual process of forgiveness, however, has often been left a mystery. Yes, it is good and helpful to let go of resentment, but how do we let go of resentment when we have been harmed? Of course it is better not to exact retribution, but how can we forgo retribution when what has been taken from us cannot be restored? And is it even possible to forgive and still pursue justice? What steps must we follow to achieve forgiveness? How do we heal all the holes in our hearts that come with being the fragile creatures we are?

The path of forgiveness is not an easy one. On this path, we must walk through the muddy shoals of hatred and anger and make our way through grief and loss to find the acceptance that is the hallmark of forgiveness. While it would be much easier to make this journey if the route were marked clearly, it is not. The boundary line between those who have caused harm and those who have been harmed is not clear either. Each of us stands at one moment as the one who has been hurt, and at the next moment as the one who is inflicting the hurt. And in the next moment we straddle the boundary, lashing out in pain and rage. We all cross these lines often. Wherever you stand, whatever you have done, whatever has been done to you, we hope this book will help you.

Together, we will explore each aspect of the Fourfold Path of forgiving: Telling the Story, Naming the Hurt, Granting Forgiveness, and Renewing or Releasing the Relationship. We invite you to join us on this healing, transformational journey. It doesn't matter whether you are having trouble moving forward from the wrongs that were done to you, or whether you need the courage to admit the wrongs you have done. Forgiveness is nothing less than the way we heal the world. We heal the world by healing each and every one of our hearts. The process is simple, but it is not easy.

I am writing this book with my daughter, Mpho, who is a fellow priest. Mpho has worked deeply with parishioners and pilgrims in their search for forgiveness and healing. She is pursuing a doctorate on the subject of forgiveness and brings a wealth of knowledge to this collaboration. She also brings a very personal story of her own journey along the Fourfold Path, and shares her struggle to understand and forgive.

This book is an invitation for you to walk with us on the path of forgiveness. In it, we will share our personal stories, along with the stories of others who have inspired us, and what we have learned about the process of forgiving. We have seen this process work to transform situations and restore relationships among family, friends, strangers, and enemies alike. We have seen it drain the venom from the small, everyday slights we can carelessly inflict on one another, and bring healing in the wake of the most brutal acts of cruelty imaginable. It is our most cherished belief that there is no one who is irredeemable, no situation that is without hope, and no crime that cannot be forgiven.

If you are seeking to forgive, we hope to point the way to freedom. We will show you how you can release a perpetrator's hold on you, and free yourself from the biting chains of resentment and anger that bind you to your experience.

If you are in need of forgiveness, it is our hope that this book will show you a clear path to freeing yourself from the shackles of your past, and help you to move forward in your life. When we witness the anguish and harm we have caused, when we ask others to forgive us and make restitution, when we forgive and restore our relationships, we return to our inherent nature.

Our nature is goodness. Yes, we do much that is bad, but our essential nature is good. If it were not, then we would not be shocked and dismayed when we harm one another. When someone does something ghastly, it makes the news because it is the exception to the rule. We live surrounded by so much love, kindness, and trust that we forget it is remarkable. Forgiveness is the way we return what has been taken from us and restore the love and kindness and trust that has been lost. With each act of forgiveness, whether small or great, we move toward wholeness. Forgiveness is nothing less than how we bring peace to ourselves and our world.

The Book of Forgiving is written, first and foremost, for those who need to forgive. We have done so because even those who need forgiveness must also forgive the harm that was done to them. This is not an excuse or a justification for what we have done, just recognition of the harm that gets passed along from hand to hand and generation to generation. No one is born a criminal; no one is born cruel. Each of us is born whole, but that wholeness can so easily be shattered.

In South Africa, we chose to seek forgiveness rather than revenge. That choice averted a bloodbath. For every injustice, there is a choice. As we have said, you can choose forgiveness or revenge, but revenge is always costly. Choosing forgiveness rather than retaliation ultimately serves to make you a stronger and freer person. Peace always comes to those who choose to forgive. While both Mpho and I have seen the effects of drinking the bitter poison of anger and resentment—seen how it corrodes and destroys from the inside out—we have also seen the sweet balm of forgiveness soothe and transform even the most virulent situations. This is why we can say there is hope.

We do not enter onto the path of forgiving blithely, nor do we travel without some trepidation that it may not go as planned. Forgiveness is a conversation, and like most important conversations, it needs a language that is clear and honest and sincere. This book will help you learn the language of forgiveness. Along the way, we will offer meditations, exercises, and rituals to guide and help you as you walk along the path. Some of the exercises will, we hope, offer comfort and solace, as well as inspire your compassion. We imagine that some of the exercises will also challenge you.

We would be guilty of false advertising if we didn't tell

you that, like all conversations, the outcome of the forgiveness process cannot be known in advance. This book is not
a cure-all or a panacea. It is our hope, however, that these
pages will guide you to the outcome you seek. We trust
that in these pages you can learn the skills and disposition of
heart you will need to repair your relationships and, in some
important way, contribute to repairing our world.

In South Africa, *Ubuntu* is our way of making sense of
the world. The word literally means "humanity." It is the
philosophy and belief that a person is only a person through
other people. In other words, we are human only in relation
to other humans. Our humanity is bound up in one another,
and any tear in the fabric of connection between us must be
repaired for us all to be made whole. This interconnectedness
is the very root of who we are.

To walk the path of forgiveness is to recognize that your
crimes harm you as they harm me. To walk the path of forgiveness is to recognize that my dignity is bound up in your
dignity, and every wrongdoing hurts us all.

Even when we recognize our interconnectedness, forgiveness can still be a difficult path to walk. Some days it will
seem as if for every one step forward we take two steps back.
It is a journey. And before the beginning of any new journey,
big or small, there must be the willingness to take that first
tentative step forward. There is a Gaelic proverb which states
"Nothing is easy for the unwilling." Without willingness,
this journey will be impossible. Before compassion comes the
willingness to feel compassion. Before transformation there
must be the belief that transformation is possible, and the

willingness to be transformed. Before forgiveness there must be the willingness to consider forgiving.

We will take this journey with you. Even if you believe there is no way you could ever forgive, or you believe that what you have done is so heinous you could never be forgiven, we will walk with you. If you are afraid or unsure or doubt that your situation could be transformed, we invite you to try. If you are without hope, paralyzed by guilt, drowning in grief, or full of anger, we invite you to come with us. We walk this path with you because we believe it is a path that will offer healing and transformation. We invite you to take this journey with us not because it will be easy but because, in the end, the path of forgiving is the only path worth taking.

Prayer Before the Prayer

I want to be willing to forgive
But I dare not ask for the will to forgive
In case you give it to me
And I am not yet ready
I am not yet ready for my heart to soften
I am not yet ready to be vulnerable again
Not yet ready to see that there is humanity in my tormentor's eyes
Or that the one who hurt me may also have cried
I am not yet ready for the journey
I am not yet interested in the path
I am at the prayer before the prayer of forgiveness
Grant me the will to want to forgive
Grant it to me not yet but soon

Can I even form the words
Forgive me?
Dare I even look?
Do I dare to see the hurt I have caused?
I can glimpse all the shattered pieces of that fragile thing
That soul trying to rise on the broken wings of hope
But only out of the corner of my eye
I am afraid of it
And if I am afraid to see
How can I not be afraid to say
Forgive me?

Is there a place where we can meet?
You and me
The place in the middle
The no man's land
Where we straddle the lines
Where you are right
And I am right too
And both of us are wrong and wronged
Can we meet there?
And look for the place where the path begins
The path that ends when we forgive

Supplies for the Journey

All journeys must be provisioned. Your journey requires two objects to support your healing:

Please get a private journal that you will use to complete the writing exercises given in each chapter. This will be your own personal "book of forgiving." It can be a plain notebook or a special journal you purchase just for this work. Only you will read this journal, and in it you should feel free and safe to record your thoughts, emotions, ideas, and progress along the Fourfold Path.

Please go out and find a stone that appeals to you on some level. It can be beautiful or ugly. It shouldn't be a pebble, nor should it be a boulder. Find a stone with some weight to it. It should be small enough to carry in the palm of your hand and large enough that you won't lose it. Note in your journal exactly where you found the stone and what it was about the stone that appealed to you.

Welcome. You have begun to walk the Fourfold Path.

Part One

UNDERSTANDING FORGIVENESS

Chapter 1

Why Forgive?

THERE WERE SO MANY NIGHTS when I, as a young boy, had to watch helplessly as my father verbally and physically abused my mother. I can still recall the smell of alcohol, see the fear in my mother's eyes, and feel the hopeless despair that comes when we see people we love hurting each other in incomprehensible ways. I would not wish that experience on anyone, especially not a child. If I dwell in those memories, I can feel myself wanting to hurt my father back, in the same ways he hurt my mother, and in ways of which I was incapable as a small boy. I see my mother's face and I see this gentle human being whom I loved so very much and who did nothing to deserve the pain inflicted upon her.

When I recall this story, I realize how difficult the process of forgiving truly is. Intellectually, I know my father caused pain because he was in pain. Spiritually, I know my faith tells me my father deserves to be forgiven as God forgives us all. But it is still difficult. The traumas we have witnessed or experienced live on in our memories. Even years later they can cause us fresh pain each time we recall them.

Are you hurt and suffering? Is the injury new, or is it an old unhealed wound? Know that what was done to you was wrong, unfair, and undeserved. You are right to be outraged. And it is perfectly normal to want to hurt back when you have been hurt. But hurting back rarely satisfies. We think it will, but it doesn't. If I slap you after you slap me, it does not lessen the sting I feel on my own face, nor does it diminish my sadness as to the fact you have struck me. Retaliation gives, at best, only momentary respite from our pain. The only way to experience healing and peace is to forgive. Until we can forgive, we remain locked in our pain and locked out of the possibility of experiencing healing and freedom, locked out of the possibility of being at peace.

Without forgiveness, we remain tethered to the person who harmed us. We are bound with chains of bitterness, tied together, trapped. Until we can forgive the person who harmed us, that person will hold the keys to our happiness; that person will be our jailor. When we forgive, we take back control of our own fate and our feelings. We become our own liberators. We don't forgive to help the other person. We don't forgive for others. We forgive for ourselves. Forgiveness, in other words, is the best form of self-interest. This is true both spiritually and scientifically.

The Science of Forgiveness

During the past decade there has been more and more research into forgiveness. Whereas previously the discussion of forgiveness was left to the religious, it is now gaining attention as an academic discipline studied not only by philosophers and theologians, but also by psychologists and physicians. There are hundreds of research projects on forgiveness taking place at universities around the world. The Campaign for Forgiveness Research, with funding from the Templeton Foundation, has forty-six different research projects on forgiveness alone.[1] Even neuroscientists are studying the biology of forgiveness and exploring evolutionary barriers in the brain that hinder the act of forgiving. Some are even looking to see if there might be a forgiveness gene somewhere in our DNA.

As modern forgiveness research evolves, the findings clearly show that forgiving transforms people mentally, emotionally, spiritually, and even physically. In *Forgive for Good: A Proven Prescription for Health and Happiness,* psychologist Fred Luskin writes, "In careful scientific studies, forgiveness training has been shown to reduce depression, increase hopefulness, decrease anger, improve spiritual connection, [and] increase emotional self-confidence."[2] These are just some of the very real and concrete psychological benefits. Research also shows that people who are more forgiving report fewer health and mental problems, and fewer physical symptoms of stress.

As more and more scientists document the healing power of forgiveness, they also look at the mentally and physically corrosive effects of not forgiving. Hanging on to anger and ntment, living in a constant state of stress, can damage the heart as well as the soul. In fact, research has shown that failure to forgive may be a risk factor for heart disease, high blood pressure, and a score of other chronic stress-related illnesses.[3] Medical and psychological studies have also shown that a person holding on to anger and resentment is at an increased risk for anxiety, depression, and insomnia, and is more likely to suffer from high blood pressure, ulcers, migraines, backaches, heart attack, and even cancer. The reverse is also true. Genuine forgiveness can transform these ailments. When stress, anxiety, and depression are reduced, so are the accompanying physical disorders.

Studies will continue to measure the heart rate, blood pressure, and longevity of those who forgive and those who don't. Journal articles will be written and, in the end, science will prove what people have known for millennia: forgiving is good for you. Health benefits are only the beginning. To forgive is also to release yourself from whatever trauma and hardship you have experienced and reclaim your life as your own.

Healing the Whole

What the medical and psychological fields cannot study, quantify, or dissect under a microscope is the deep connection we have with one another and the drive within each of us to live in harmony.

Science is perhaps beginning to recognize what we in Africa have long known, that we are truly interdependent, even though science cannot yet fully explain our need of each other. Dr. Lisa Berkman, chair of the Department of Society, Human Development and Health at the Harvard School of Public Health, studied seven thousand men and women. According to her findings, people who were socially isolated were three times more likely to die prematurely than those who had a strong social web. Even more astonishing to the researchers, those who had a strong social circle and unhealthy lifestyle (smoking, obesity, and lack of exercise) actually lived longer than those who had a weak social circle but a healthy lifestyle.[4] A separate article in the journal *Science* concluded that loneliness was a greater risk factor for disease and death than smoking.[5] In other words, loneliness can kill you faster than cigarettes. We are deeply connected to one another whether we recognize it or not. We need each other. We evolved this way, and our survival still depends upon it.

When we are uncaring, when we lack compassion, when we are unforgiving, we will always pay the price for it. It is not, however, we alone who suffer. Our whole community suffers, and ultimately our whole world suffers. We are made to exist in a delicate network of interdependence. We are sisters and brothers, whether we like it or not. To treat anyone as if they were less than human, less than a brother or a sister, no matter what they have done, is to contravene the very laws of our humanity. And those who shred the web of interconnectedness cannot escape the consequences of their actions.

In my own family, sibling squabbles have spilled into intergenerational alienations. When adult siblings refuse to speak to each other because of some offense, recent or long past, their children and grandchildren can lose out on the joy of strong family relationships. The children and grand-children may never know what occasioned the freeze. They know only that "We don't visit this aunt" or "We don't really know those cousins." Forgiveness among the members of older generations could open the door to healthy and supportive relationships among younger generations.

If your own well-being—your physical, emotional, and mental health—is not enough, if your life and your future are not enough, then perhaps you will forgive for the benefit of those you love, the family that is precious to you. Anger and bitterness do not just poison you, they poison all your relationships, including those with your children.

The Freedom of Forgiveness

Forgiveness is not dependent on the actions of others. Yes, it is certainly easier to offer forgiveness when the perpetrator expresses remorse and offers some sort of reparation or restitution. Then, you can feel as if you have been paid back in some way. You can say, "I am willing to forgive you for stealing my pen, and after you give me my pen back, I shall forgive you." This is the most familiar pattern of forgiveness. In this understanding, forgiveness is something we offer to another, a gift we bestow upon someone, but it is a gift that has strings attached.

The problem is that the strings we attach to the gift of forgiveness become the chains that bind us to the person who harmed us. Those are chains to which the perpetrator holds the key. We may set the conditions for granting our forgiveness, but the person who harmed us decides whether or not the conditions are too onerous to fulfill. We continue to be that person's victim. "I will not speak to you until you say you are sorry!" my young granddaughter, Onalenna, will rage. Her older sister, thinking the demand unfair and unjustified, refuses to apologize. The two remain locked together in a battle of wills bound by mutual resentment. There are two routes out of the impasse: the older Nyaniso can apologize, or Onalenna can decide to forgo the apology and forgive unconditionally.

Unconditional forgiveness is a different model of forgiveness than the gift with strings. This is forgiveness as a grace, a free gift freely given. In this model, forgiveness frees the person who inflicted the harm from the weight of the victim's whim—what the victim may demand in order to grant forgiveness—and the victim's threat of vengeance. But it also frees the one who forgives. The one who offers forgiveness as a grace is immediately untethered from the yoke that bound him or her to the person who caused the harm. When you forgive, you are free to move on in life, to grow, to no longer be a victim. When you forgive, you slip the yoke, and your future is unshackled from your past.

In South Africa, the logic of apartheid created enmity among the races. Some of the poisonous effects of that system still linger. But forgiveness has opened the door to a different future for us, one that is not bound by the logic of our past. Earlier this year I sat in the sun enjoying the delighted shrieks of a gaggle of seven-year-old girls celebrating my granddaughter's birthday. They represented every race of our rainbow nation. Their future is not determined by the logic of apartheid. Race is not the basis upon which they will choose their friends, build their families, select their careers, or decide where to live. Their future is being charted by the logic of a new South Africa and the grace of forgiveness. The new South Africa is a country that is being created because, laying down the burden of years of prejudice, oppression, brutality, and torture, some extraordinary ordinary people had the courage to forgive.

Our Shared Humanity

Ultimately, forgiveness is a choice we make, and the ability to forgive others comes from the recognition that we are all flawed and all human. We all have made mistakes and harmed others. We will again. We find it easier to practice forgiveness when we can recognize that the roles could have been reversed. Each of us could have been the perpetrator rather than the victim. Each of us has the capacity to commit the wrongs against others that were committed against us. Although I might say, "I would never . . ." genuine humility will answer, "Never say never." Rather say, "I hope that, given the same set of circumstances, I would not . . ." But can we ever really know?

As we explained in the introduction, we have written this book because, truthfully, this is not a dichotomy. No person will always stand in the camp of the perpetrator. No person will always be the one who is the victim. In some situations we have been harmed, and in others we have harmed. And sometimes we straddle both camps, as when, in the heat of a marital spat, we trade hurts with our partners. Not all harms are equivalent, but this is really not the issue. Those who wish to compare how much they have wronged to how much they have been wronged will find themselves drowning in a whirlpool of victimization and denial. Those who think they are beyond reproach have not taken an honest look in the mirror.

People are not born hating each other and wishing to cause harm. It is a learned condition. Children do not dream of growing up to be rapists or murderers, and yet every rapist and every murderer was once a child. And there are times when I look at some of those who are described as "monsters" and I honestly believe that there, but for the grace of God, go I. I do not say this because I am some singular saint. I say this because I have sat with condemned men on death row, I have spoken with former police officers who have admitted inflicting the cruelest torture, I have visited child soldiers who have committed acts of nauseating depravity, and I have recognized in each of them a depth of humanity that was a mirror of my own.

Forgiveness is truly the grace by which we enable another person to get up, and get up with dignity, to begin anew. To not forgive leads to bitterness and hatred. Like self-hatred and self-contempt, hatred of others gnaws away at our vitals. Whether hatred is projected out or stuffed in, it is always corrosive to the human spirit.

Forgiveness Is Not a Luxury

Forgiveness is not some airy-fairy thing. It has to do with the real world. Healing and reconciliation are not magic spells. They do not erase the reality of an injury. To forgive is not to pretend that what happened did not happen. Healing does not draw a veil over the hurt. Rather, healing and reconciliation demand an honest reckoning. For Christians, Jesus Christ sets the pattern for forgiveness and reconciliation. He offered his betrayers forgiveness. Jesus, the Son of God, could erase the signs of leprosy; heal those broken in body, mind, or spirit; and restore sight to the blind. He must also have been able to obliterate the signs of the torture and death he endured. But he chose not to erase that evidence. After the resurrection, he appeared to his disciples. In most instances, he showed them his wounds and his scars. This is what healing demands. Behavior that is hurtful, shameful, abusive, or demeaning must be brought into the fierce light of truth. And truth can be brutal. In fact, truth may exacerbate the hurt; it might make things worse. But if we want real forgiveness and real healing, we must face the real injury.

The Invitation to Forgive

In the chapters that follow, we will take a deeper look at forgiveness. We will examine what it is not and what it truly is. For now, it is enough to say that the invitation to forgive is not an invitation to forget. Nor is it an invitation to claim that an injury is less hurtful than it really is. Nor is it a request to paper over the fissure in a relationship, to say it's okay when it's not. It's not okay to be injured. It's not okay to be abused. It's not okay to be violated. It's not okay to be betrayed.

The invitation to forgive is an invitation to find healing and peace. In my native language, Xhosa, one asks forgiveness by saying, "*Ndicel' uxolo*" (I ask for peace). The locution is quite beautiful and deeply perceptive. Forgiveness opens the door to peace between people and opens the space for peace within each person. The victim cannot have peace without forgiving. The perpetrator will not have genuine peace while unforgiven. There cannot be peace between victim and perpetrator while the injury lies between them. The invitation to forgive is an invitation to search out the perpetrator's humanity. When we forgive, we recognize the reality that there, but for the grace of God, go I.

If I traded lives with my father, if I had experienced the stresses and pressures my father faced, if I had to bear the burdens he bore, would I have behaved as he did? I do not know. I hope I would have been different, but I do not know.

My father has long since died, but if I could speak to him today, I would want to tell him that I had forgiven him. What would I say to him? I would begin by thanking him for all the wonderful things he did for me as my father, but then I would tell him that there was this one thing that hurt me very much. I would tell him how what he did to my mother affected me, how it pained me.

Perhaps he would hear me out; perhaps he would not. But still I would forgive him. Since I cannot speak to him, I have had to forgive him in my heart. If my father were here today, whether he asked for forgiveness or not, and even if he refused to admit that what he had done was wrong or could not explain why he had done what he did, I would still forgive him. Why would I do such a thing? I would walk the path of forgiveness with him because I know it is the only way to heal the pain in my boyhood heart. Forgiving my father frees me. When I no longer hold his offenses against him, my memory of him no longer exerts any control over my moods or my disposition. His violence and my inability to protect my mother no longer define me. I am not the small boy cowering in fear of his drunken rage. I have a new and different story. Forgiveness has liberated both of us. We are free.

Forgiveness takes practice, honesty, open-mindedness, and a willingness (even if it is a weary willingness) to try. This healing journey is not a primer—a book that we must read and understand. This healing journey is a practice—something in which we must participate. It is our own path to forgiveness. To truly forgive, we must have a better understanding of forgiveness, but first we must understand what forgiveness is not. We will explore this in the next chapter.

Before we move on, let us pause to listen to what the heart hears.

I will forgive you
The words are so small
But there is a universe hidden in them
When I forgive you
All those cords of resentment pain and sadness that had wrapped
themselves around my heart will be gone
When I forgive you
You will no longer define me
You measured me and assessed me and
decided that you could hurt me
I didn't count
But I will forgive you
Because I do count
I do matter
I am bigger than the image you have of me

I am stronger
I am more beautiful
And I am infinitely more precious than you thought me
I will forgive you
My forgiveness is not a gift that I am giving to you
When I forgive you
My forgiveness will be a gift that gives itself to me

Summary
Why Forgive

- Forgiveness is beneficial to our health.
- Forgiveness offers freedom from the past, from a perpetrator, from future victimization.
- Forgiveness heals families and communities.
- We forgive so we don't suffer, physically or mentally, the corrosive effects of holding on to anger and resentment.
- We are all interconnected and have a shared humanity.
- Forgiveness is a gift we give to ourselves.

Meditation

Opening to the Light

1. Close your eyes and follow your breath.
2. When you feel centered, imagine yourself in a safe place; this may be indoors or outdoors, whichever feels safest to you.
3. In the center of your safe space is a box with many drawers.
4. The drawers are labeled. The inscriptions show hurts you have yet to forgive.
5. Choose a drawer and open it. Rolled or folded or crumpled up inside it are all the thoughts and feelings the incident evokes.
6. You can choose to empty out this drawer.
7. Bring your hurt into the light and examine it.
8. Unfold the resentment you have felt and set it aside.
9. Smooth out the ache and let it drift up into the sunlight and disappear.
10. If any feeling seems too big or too unbearable, set it aside to look at later.
11. When the drawer is empty, sit for a moment with it on your lap.
12. Then remove the label from this drawer.
13. As the label comes off, you will see the drawer turn to sand. The wind will sweep it away. You don't need it anymore.
14. There will be no space left for that hurt in the box. That space is not needed anymore.
15. If there are more drawers still to be emptied, you can repeat this meditation now or later.

Stone Ritual

Carrying the Stone

1. You will need your palm-size stone.
2. For the space of one morning (approximately six hours) hold the stone in your non-dominant hand. Do not set the stone down for any reason during this period.
3. At the end of six hours, proceed to the journal exercise.

Journal Exercise

1. What did you notice about carrying the stone?
2. When did you notice it the most?
3. Did it hinder any of your activities?
4. Was it ever useful?
5. In what ways was carrying the stone like carrying an unforgiven hurt?
6. Make a list of the people you need to forgive in your life.
7. Make another list of all those you would like to have forgive you.

Chapter 2

What Forgiveness Is Not

IN AN INSTANT, life can change. For Mpho, that instant was in April 2012:

I still can't describe my own feelings fully. Nausea, disgust, fear, confusion, and grief overwhelmed me. Our housekeeper, Angela, lay on the floor of my daughter's room. The blood from her brutalized body pooled around her. Yes, the medics confirmed shortly afterward, she was dead. She had been dead for some hours. The days and weeks that followed were a blur of a life upended. The blood and the body are gone, but the event continues to reverberate in our lives.

We miss her. In a few short months, she had made her mark on our lives. Her quirks and her kindness had become a part of our story and our family. Her laughter had filled our home. Her strange turns of phrase had become part of our language. Her absence is a sad, scary shadow. Weeping and nightmares, terrors and sleeplessness, brittle silences and nerve-shattering sounds—all of these have become a part of our new reality. The home we had shared is no longer home. We cannot live there. "Was anything stolen?" the young policeman asked. A life was stolen. No, more than one life was stolen. There was one dead body, but so many lives were changed irrevocably, snatched away, stolen. So many lives and one happy home gone. Sometimes I feel sad for the murderer, unutterably sad. At other times I feel angry. How could anyone be so vile? How could any person be so brutal? Why Angela? What harm had she done anyone? How dare anyone violate my home? There are moments when the anger turns to rage, and there are moments when I want to strike back!

In one unexpected act of violence and rage, we can experience horror and loss so great we don't think we can survive. We see it on the evening news: children go missing, either never to be found or their bodies are found discarded like the day's trash. We read about it in the newspaper: the torture and rape of women caught in the crossfire of civil war. We see it on the Internet: classrooms and movie theaters where innocent people are shot at indiscriminately, killed tragically, violently, and senselessly. We hear reports of drive-by shootings and home invasions, gangs retaliating against gangs, and deaths avenged by more deaths. We watch and read and listen, but we do all this from a distance and with a sad detachment at the horrors people are capable of inflicting upon one another.

Then it happens to us. And the horror we once watched from a distance, as if it were a movie or a play, is now in our homes and in our classrooms and in our neighborhoods.

In our own families.

There are times when Mpho cannot imagine ever forgiving the person who brought such horror into her home; the person who forever and indelibly marked her daughters' psyches and childhoods with a singular and senseless act of brutality and bloodshed. I tell you this because even for people of faith, who believe in unconditional forgiveness, even for people like Mpho and me—people who dare to write books about forgiveness—forgiveness is not easy. It is not easy for Mpho. It is not easy for me. And it is understandable if forgiveness does not come easily for you.

Forgiveness Is Not Weakness

We all aspire to be forgiving people. We admire and esteem those who find it in their hearts to forgive, even when they are betrayed, cheated, stolen from, lied to, or worse. The parents who forgive the person who murdered their child inspire in us something like awe. The woman who can forgive her rapist seems possessed of a special kind of courage. A man forgives the people who tortured him brutally, and we think his deed heroic. Do we see these people and these acts and think those who forgive are weak? We do not. Forgiveness is not weak. It is not passive. It is not for the faint of heart.

Forgiving does not mean being spineless, nor does it mean one doesn't get angry. I get angry, mostly when I see others being harmed or when I see the rights of others being trampled underfoot. I have known people who have been able to be compassionate and forgiving, even under the most strenuous circumstances while undergoing the most horrific treatment. Bishop Malusi Mpumlwana is someone like that. Arrested as an anti-apartheid activist, he endured excruciating physical torture at the hands of the South African police. His experience renewed his commitment to anti-apartheid work. He did not work out of thirst for revenge. He told me that, in the midst of his torture, he had an astonishing insight: "These are God's children and they are losing their humanity. We have to help them recover it." It is a remarkable feat to be able to see past the inhumanity of the behavior and recognize the humanity of the person committing the atrocious acts. This is not weakness. This is heroic strength, the noblest strength of the human spirit.

At the age of twelve, Bassam Aramin watched as another boy his age was shot and killed by an Israeli soldier. In that moment, he felt a "deep need for revenge" and joined a group of freedom fighters in Hebron. Some called him a terrorist, but he felt he was fighting for his safety, his home, and his right to be free. At seventeen, he was caught planning an attack on Israeli troops and sentenced to seven years in prison. In prison, he only learned to hate more as he was stripped naked and beaten by his prison guards. "They were beating us without hatred, because for them this was just a training exercise and they saw us as objects."

While in prison, Bassam engaged in a dialogue with his Israeli guard. Each thought the other was the "terrorist" and each equally denied being the "settler" in the land they shared. Through their conversations, they realized how much they had in common with the other. For Bassam, it was the first time he recalls feeling empathy in his life.

Seeing the transformation that took place between him and his captor, as they recognized their shared humanity, Bassam realized that violence could never bring peace. This realization changed his life.

In 2005, Bassam Aramin cofounded a group called Combatants for Peace. He has not picked up a weapon since, and for Bassam this is not a sign of weakness but of true strength. In 2007, Bassam's ten-year-old daughter, Abir, was shot by an Israeli soldier as she stood outside her school. Bassam says, "Abir's murder could have led me down the easy path of hatred and vengeance, but for me there was no return from dialogue and nonviolence. After all, it was one Israeli soldier who shot my daughter, but one hundred former Israeli soldiers who built a garden in her name at the school where she was murdered."[6]

I say again, forgiveness is not weakness.

Forgiveness Is Not a Subversion of Justice

There are those who believe an injustice can be made right only when someone is made to pay for the harm they have caused. Forgiveness, they say, subverts the course of justice. The truth is that people will always live with the consequences of their actions. In some cases, the forgiveness offered by the injured party comes after the perpetrator has completed his or her penance. This was so in Northern Ireland. In 2006, the BBC aired a documentary series, *Facing the Truth,* that brought together victims and perpetrators of Northern Ireland's violent conflict. What was remarkable about this process was that, unlike the South African Truth and Reconciliation Commission, the series had no power to grant amnesty to the perpetrators. In fact, the perpetrators who came forward seeking forgiveness had already been tried and convicted for their crimes. They had already completed their prison sentences. But still they came. They did not come to change the past or to challenge justice. They came to seek forgiveness.

Even the Christian God does not subvert temporal justice to open the door to eternal forgiveness and peace. The thief who hung on the cross next to Jesus was the only person to be promised paradise. He died on a cross for his crimes. He lives in eternity for his repentance.

Even when perpetrators are granted amnesty and immunity from prosecution, as in South Africa's TRC process, they cannot be considered to have "gotten away scot-free." In standing before the commission to speak their deeds, they forever changed the status they held in their families and their communities. After years of hiding their activities, they had to stand up in a public place and tell the truth of their cruelty, callousness, and murderous actions. Yes, they were granted amnesty, but justice was not subverted in the hearts of the many victims and their families who needed to know the truth.

Often, even after "justice" is served, so many people find that the story hasn't ended, and no one has found a route to a new beginning. Forgiveness is the only way out of the trap that injury creates.

Forgiveness Is Not Forgetting

Some find forgiveness difficult because they believe forgiving means forgetting the pain they have suffered. I can say unequivocally that forgiving does not mean forgetting the harm. It does not mean denying the harm. It does not mean pretending the harm did not happen or the injury was not as bad as it really was. Quite the opposite is true. The cycle of forgiveness can be activated and completed only in absolute truth and honesty.

Forgiving requires giving voice to the violations and naming the pains we have suffered. Forgiving does not require that we carry our suffering in silence or be martyrs on a cross of lies. Forgiveness does not mean that we pretend things are anything other than they are. *I am hurt,* we say. *I am betrayed,* we announce. *I am in pain and grief. I have been treated unfairly. I am feeling ashamed. I am angry this has been done to me. I am sad and I am lost. I may never forget what you have done to me, but I will forgive. I will do everything in my power not to let you harm me again. I will not retaliate against you or against myself.*

If there is a pattern of hurt from the perpetrator, then each instance of harm is not discrete. There is history, and we are not served by forgetting our history. There is always a risk when we forgive that everything will not turn out all right. Just as we take a leap of faith when we make a commitment to love someone and get married, we also take a leap of faith when we commit ourselves to a practice of forgiving. We do not forget or deny that we are always vulnerable to being hurt again, but we leap anyway.

Forgiveness Is Not Easy

Often when we are suffering from loss or harm of some kind, forgiving can seem too overwhelming, too complicated, to even consider. How do we forgive if there has been no apology or explanation for why someone has hurt us so? How do we think of forgiving when we feel the person has not done anything to "deserve" our forgiveness? Where do we even start?

The work of forgiveness is not easy. Perhaps you have already tried to forgive someone and just couldn't do it. Perhaps you have forgiven and the person did not show remorse or change his or her behavior or own up to his or her offenses—and you find yourself unforgiving all over again.

Forgiveness is not an effortless act for any of us, and it does not serve anyone to minimize the complexity involved in the work of forgiving. It is best to break our forgiving down into bite-size pieces, and begin from wherever we are standing. Tell your story for as long as you need to. Name your hurts until they no longer pierce your heart. Grant forgiveness when you are ready to let go of a past that cannot be changed. Reconcile or release the relationship as you choose.

Forgiving is not easy, but it is the path to healing. It was not easy for Nelson Mandela to spend twenty-seven years in prison, but when people say to me what a waste it was, I say no, it was not a waste. It took twenty-seven years for him to be transformed from an angry, unforgiving young radical into an icon of reconciliation, forgiveness, and honor who could go on to lead a country back from the brink of civil war and self-destruction.

Our suffering, our pain, and our losses have the power to transform us. It does not always feel just, nor is it easy, but we have seen that, with time, great good can come from great sorrow. In the next chapter, we will begin to explore the Fourfold Path of forgiveness.

But first, let us pause to listen to what the heart hears.

God forgives unconditionally
So can we
The thief on the cross still dies on his cross
But forgiveness will set his spirit free
And what of you and me standing on the ground with our piles
of hurts mounting so high
Will we die a thousand deaths before we die?
Yearning for revenge, will we die of that thirst?
Will the rage that fills us be the stake on which we burn?
Will we stumble over every resistance placed in our way?
And stay stuck in the misery of it all?
Or will we take the chance that we might break free by following
this path where it leads
Past the whys and lies about how it cannot be
Here is our chance
Take this chance
Break free

Summary
What Forgiveness Is Not

- Forgiveness is not easy—it requires hard work and a consistent willingness.
- Forgiveness is not weakness—it requires courage and strength.
- Forgiveness does not subvert justice—it creates space for justice to be enacted with a purity of purpose that does not include revenge.
- Forgiveness is not forgetting—it requires a fearless remembering of hurt.
- Forgiveness is not quick—it can take several journeys through the cycles of remembering and grief before one can truly forgive and be free.

Meditation

Sitting in the Safe Space

Sometimes the work of forgiveness feels too much like work and all you want to do is be still and feel safe. For this meditation you will create a cloak of safety that will always be within reach.

1. Begin by sitting comfortably. If you choose, close your eyes lightly.

2. Pay attention to your breath. Don't direct it. Follow it.

3. When you have settled into the rhythm of your breath, allow yourself to feel a cloak of safety surrounding you like a fabric.

4. What is the texture of this cloak? Does it have a color? Does it have a fragrance?

5. Settle into this cloak. Does it feel warm or cool?

6. Describe this cloak in your imagination as fully as you are able. Pull the cloak around you and settle into feeling safe.

7. When you feel the need for this cloak of safety, know it is always there and you can just reach for it.

Stone Ritual

Tracing the Myths

1. Take your stone. Set it on a sheet of paper in your journal and trace around it.
2. Make five tracings of your stone.
3. Inside each tracing write one thing that forgiveness is not. Forgiveness is not:
   a. weakness
   b. injustice
   c. forgetting
   d. easy
   e. quick
4. For each of these myths about forgiveness, call to mind an instance where that myth is holding you back from granting forgiveness.

Journal Exercise

Forgiving is a process of letting go.

1. Think of the things you must give up or let go of in order to forgive.

2. The list might include things like the right to revenge or the expectation of an apology. It might even include having to give up an expectation that the person who hurt you will understand the pain they have caused.

3. As you jot down this list, pause with each item and offer thanks for the ability to let go of what you do not need in order to forgive.

Chapter 3

Understanding the Fourfold Path

MPHO MET HER IN THE HOSPITAL. She was a pretty girl, just into her teenage years. She had been found sleeping in the girls' bathroom at her school. After days of sitting in stubborn silence, while the nurses plied her with candy and forbidden soft drinks, she started to speak. The story tumbled out over shards of rage, fear, and betrayal. After years alone, her mom had remarried. At first, the man was nice. He was nice to her mom. He was nice to her. And then he was too nice to her. And then it was just horrible. She tried to tell her mom. But her mom already knew. What would they live on if this man was imprisoned or gone?

"You can't tell. Don't dare tell."

Fear and betrayal drove her out of her home. Rage shut

her mouth and kept her locked in that stubborn silence. After the first telling, she retold the story again and again, speaking her pain and grief, wearing a path through her own fear. How could that man do this to her? How could her mother fail to protect her? At first, her feelings seemed to harden into a tight ball of hurt and anger. With time, as she talked, she seemed to look beyond her own rage and anguish and see her mother's fear and shame. What the mother had endured didn't make what the girl had suffered okay. But as she started to recognize something of her mother's experience, the hard ball of rage began to soften and uncoil. She was beginning to forgive.

After understanding what forgiveness is not, we must look deeply at what forgiveness is and the actual process of forgiving. None of us wants to have our life story be the sum of all the ways we have been hurt. We are not created to live in suffering and isolation. We are created to live in love and connection with one another. When there is a break in that connection, we must have a method of repair.

The method we offer is what we call the Fourfold Path. The first step on the path is Telling the Story; then comes Naming the Hurt, Granting Forgiveness, and finally, Renewing or Releasing the Relationship. Forgiveness is not new, and what we describe is what humans have been doing throughout history in every culture on the planet. The Fourfold Path probably goes back to Adam and Eve and that pesky apple. Yes, humans have been having to forgive each other for as long as we've been human.

Retaliate or Reconnect

Evolutionary biologists suggest that we are hardwired to seek revenge and hurt back when we are hurt. This is how our ancestors survived when confronted by a threat, and this is our nature now in response to a threat. What can we do but retaliate when it is in our genes? If we are hit hard, we must hit back harder. As Darwin said, it is survival of the fittest.

But is this true? There is no doubt that revenge is part of our evolutionary biology, but there is also no doubt that we are hardwired to forgive and reconnect. Primatologists show that even monkeys seek to make amends. They extend their hands to one another and become very agitated when the group is not in harmony. For humans, "sorry" joins "please" and "thank you" among the earliest additions to a child's vocabulary. This thirst for harmony is why our hearts soar when we hear that someone who has been wronged has chosen to forgive. This is why the stories we have shared in this book resonate so deeply. Somewhere in our heart of hearts we know that forgiveness is truly the gateway to harmony and peace.

The fact that we have an impulse toward revenge does not equate to a moral justification to hurt back when we are hurt. Just because we have an action hardwired in our brains does not mean we are justified in indulging in this action. We have impulses for aggression in many contexts, but we know we must not act on them. We have impulses for sex, but we understand that acting on those impulses is not always appropriate, so we contain ourselves. Although we are hardwired for revenge and aggression, scientists have also shown that we are hardwired for connection. Our brains want us to connect

with other people; indeed ostracism or shunning—a refusal
to connect—has long been a form of punishment individuals and communities impose on those who arouse their ire.
Scientists are now studying mirror neurons, the mechanisms
in our brains that enable us to feel what others are feeling.[7]
We are social creatures, and our physical survival is just as
dependent on happy relationships and social connections as it
is on food, air, and water. Although this is all true, I recognize that this doesn't make forgiving any easier when you're
miserable and in pain or when your world has been upended
by a random and undeserved act of violence or cruelty.

Whenever we are injured, we face the choice of whether
to retaliate or reconnect. When we seek retaliation or
revenge, it does not satisfy us; in the sentiment of Mahatma
Gandhi, when we practice the law of an eye for an eye, we
all end up blind. If someone insults me and I, in turn, insult
him, it does not give me satisfaction. As we've said earlier,
retaliation does not lessen the sting of the first insult or take
it away. A part of me knows this is not how I should respond,
and it does not feel good when I respond in kind. There is a
certain kind of dignity we admire, and to which we aspire,
in the person who refuses to meet anger with anger, violence
with violence, or hatred with hatred.

Let us try to understand how we get drawn into a cycle of
revenge and rupture, and how we can instead choose a cycle
of forgiveness and healing—what we call the Forgiveness
Cycle. We have seen how these two impulses, one toward
retaliation and the other toward reconnection, wrestle in our
hearts. It may help for us to look in detail at this moment
of choice, the instant in which we choose to either walk the

path of revenge and be bound to suffering, or take the path of forgiveness and be freed into healing. Refer to the following diagram to see a visual portrayal of the process we are describing:

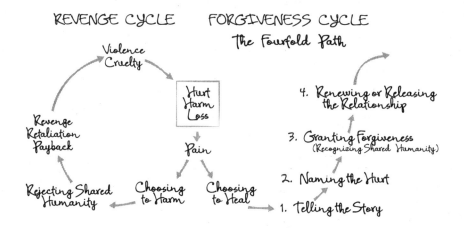

Inevitably, because we are fragile and vulnerable creatures, we experience some hurt, harm, or loss. The wound can be physical, emotional, or psychosocial. We can be hurt with a weapon or a word. We can be slighted, rejected, or betrayed. Donna Hicks, in her marvelous book *Dignity,* tells us that all of these harms are affronts to our physical, emotional, or social dignity. There is no way of living with other people without, at some point, being hurt. This hurt is what puts us on the cycle. I suppose God could have made us creatures who were indifferent to the actions of others, but that is not how we are. I suppose we could have evolved differently. We could need no one and care for no one, but this is not the path our evolution has taken.

The response to hurt is universal. Each of us will experience sadness, pain, anger, or shame, or a combination of any or all of these. Now comes the moment of choice, although for most of us our reactions are so habitual we don't even realize we have a choice. What so often happens is that we step unawares into the Revenge Cycle. The affront is so painful, so intolerable, that we cannot accept it, and instead of placing our hands on our hearts and weeping for what we have lost, we point our fingers or shake our fists at the one who has harmed us. Instead of embracing our sadness, we stoke our anger. We feel compelled to restore our dignity by rejecting our pain and denying our grief. That rejection places us in the closed loop of the Revenge Cycle.

I have had this experience. A few years ago I was given an award by an American charity. The ceremony was held at a swanky Washington, DC, hotel. The emcee was a noted American actress. The morning after the event, I was sitting in the hotel lobby waiting for my hosts to usher me to a series of meetings. I was wearing my usual dark-suited clerical garb, including a purple shirt, clergy collar, and a pectoral cross. My signature Greek fisherman's cap was in my hand. A young lad from the hotel bell-staff approached me: "Are you [Ms. Famous Emcee's] driver?" Before I had a moment to fully register the question, I was taken aback. My thoughts rode the tide of feelings. Did the youth only take in that I was a black man of a certain age in a suit with a cap? Did it not occur to him that a chauffeur would wait outside near the car? Were I white and dressed the same way would he have posed the same question? My dignity was certainly assaulted. I wanted to strike back, haul this insolent boy to his manager, and take him down the peg or two he had taken me down. I wanted to push away my sense of affront.

I didn't want to admit to the sad, vulnerable place where the hurt had landed.

When we cannot admit our own woundedness, we cannot see the other as a wounded person who has harmed us out of his or her own ignorance, pain, or brokenness. We must reject our commonality. We move along the Revenge Cycle to rejecting our shared humanity. Without this recognition of our shared humanity, the bond between us frays and the social fabric tears. It is then a very short step to demanding revenge. To buy back our dignity, we think we must pay back in kind. We retaliate. Retaliation, in turn, leads to more hurt, more harm, and more loss, which keeps the Revenge Cycle going without end. There are families, tribes, and nations that have been trapped in this Revenge Cycle for generations.

While revenge may be a natural impulse, we do not have to follow its siren call. There is another way, which we call the Forgiveness Cycle. It begins after a hurt, harm, or loss at the same moment of sadness, anger, and shame we all experience. Instead of rejecting our pain and grief, in the Forgiveness Cycle we accept our pain and grief. If it is a small slight to our dignity or a small harm we have experienced from a spouse, this might be the end of it, and we might be able to forgive that person quite quickly and easily. However, if we have been hurt deeply or have lost someone or something that is precious to us, this part of the Forgiveness Cycle may be intense and long. In the coming chapters we will discuss the steps in this process in more detail.

As the young girl whose story opened this chapter discovered, by telling our stories and naming our hurt we are able to face our suffering. Rather than rejecting our pain and grief, as we did in the Revenge Cycle, we are able to acknowledge and accept these feelings. When the wound is deep, the space between our initial sadness and a full acceptance of our pain is a journey through the stages of grief—denial, anger, bargaining, depression, and ultimately acceptance. The stages of grief do not come in any prescribed order and often circle back on one another as we experience waves of loss and hurt. When we face into and accept our pain, we start to recognize that we don't have to stay stuck in our story.

The person who injured us also has a story. They have wounded us because they have stood inside their own story and acted out of pain, shame, or ignorance. They have ignored our shared humanity. When we see pain in this way, we are able to see our common bond. We might even be able to empathize with the perpetrator. We can begin to let go of our identity as a victim and their identity as a perpetrator.

This was so for the girl Mpho met in the hospital; as she began to accept her pain, she started to see her mother's pain and fear. It was so for me too; as I accepted the place in me left raw by the realities of racism and apartheid, I could see the visual shorthand that prompted the bellman's mistake. It is so for both small slights and large hurts. When we accept our own pain, we can begin to see past it to the other person's woundedness. We can begin to consider that if we were in their shoes, if we stood inside their story, we might have done to them, or to others, what they did to us. We may loathe and lament what they have done to us, or to those we love, but somehow we are able to separate the person from what he or she has done. In short, by accepting our vulnerability, we accept the perpetrator's. By accepting our humanity, we accept the perpetrator's.

When we can accept both our humanity and the perpetrator's, we can write a new story, one in which we are no longer cast as a victim but as a survivor, even perhaps a hero. In this new story, we are able to learn and grow from what has happened to us. We may even be able to use our pain as an impulse to reduce the pain and suffering of others. This is when we know we are healed. Healing does not mean reversing. Healing does not mean that what happened will never again cause us to hurt. It does not mean we will never miss those who have been lost to us or that which was taken from us. Healing means that our dignity is restored and we are able to move forward in our lives.

How Long Does It Take to Forgive?

I wish I knew the answer to that question, but no one can answer it for anyone else. Forgiveness can be quite short, happening in a matter of minutes, or it can take years to travel the Fourfold Path. It very much depends on the nature of the hurt and the unique story of situation and emotion. No one has the right to tell you how quickly you should walk this path. All we can say is that the path awaits you when you are ready. In the coming chapters, we will discuss each of these vital four steps: Telling the Story, Naming the Hurt, Granting Forgiveness, and Renewing or Releasing the Relationship. For those who come to these pages because they need to be forgiven, chapter 8 will address the complementary steps for needing forgiveness from another. Yet, as we have said from the start, everyone who has harmed another has also been harmed. We strongly recommend that you first walk the Fourfold Path to find forgiveness in your heart for the people who have harmed you. As you walk the path with the intention to forgive, you will come to understand more deeply the gift you are asking of and bestowing upon another when you ask a person to forgive what you have done. The power of this practice, the power of this path, is that we heal both as we forgive and as we are forgiven. We heal as we forgive others and as we forgive ourselves.

Forgiveness feels as if a weight has been lifted off you and you are free to let go of the past and move forward in your life. It may not be found in a single act of grace or a simple string of words, but rather in a process of truth and reconciliation.

Linda Biehl, the mother of murdered Fulbright scholar Amy Biehl, spoke of meeting and then working in the Amy Biehl Foundation with the men who killed her daughter. "I have forgiven them," she says. "Every day I wake up and my daughter is dead. Most days I wake up and I have to face her killers. Some days I have to forgive them all over again."

The Fourfold Path is a conversation that begins with a personal choice to heal and be free, a choice to seek peace and create a new story. We sit in the midst of our hurt and loss, and we face the choice of which path to take: retribution or reconciliation. We can choose to harm or we can choose to heal. It does not matter how long we have carried our suffering or how briefly. It does not matter whether the other person is contrite or remorseless. It does not matter if the one who harmed us does not acknowledge or admit the harm. It does not matter if we believe that person has not paid for his or her crimes against us, because, as we have said, forgiveness is not a choice you make for someone else; it is a choice you make for yourself.

In the Truth and Reconciliation Commission, I saw over and over again how people courageously, nobly, magnificently chose the path of forgiveness. Any of those victims could have chosen to continue the cycle of violence and retaliation, but instead they chose to seek the truth, face their grief, and recognize both their own humanity and that of the perpetrators who had so grievously harmed them. They chose the difficult path of forgiveness. Forgiveness is rarely easy, but it is always possible.

Are Some People Beyond Forgiveness?

What about evil, you may ask? Aren't some people just evil, just monsters, and aren't such people just unforgivable? I do believe there are monstrous and evil acts, but I do not believe those who commit such acts are monsters or evil. To relegate someone to the level of monster is to deny that person's ability to change and to take away that person's accountability for his or her actions and behavior. In January 2012, in Modimolle, an agricultural town in Limpopo province, South Africa, a man named Johan Kotze committed acts of monstrous and evil proportions. Indeed, such was the horror of his acts, the newspapers and town dubbed him "The Monster of Modimolle."

I was appalled at the story I read. We were all appalled. Johan Kotze was alleged to have forced three laborers at gunpoint to gang-rape and mutilate his estranged wife. He then tied her up and forced her to listen and watch as he shot and killed her son. Johan Kotze claimed he was driven to commit these horrific crimes because he saw his estranged wife with another man and, in his rage, he chose the path of revenge.

These are, without doubt, barbaric and dastardly deeds. They are acts so monstrous we are all quite right to condemn them. What shook me deeply as I read the media coverage of this case was that the righteous outrage at the alleged acts of Mr. Kotze had led journalists to call him a monster. In response, I wrote a letter to *The Star* newspaper. In it I argued that while he may indeed be guilty of inhuman, ghastly, and monstrous deeds, he is not a monster. We are actually letting him off lightly by calling him a monster, because monsters have no moral sense of right and wrong and therefore cannot be held morally culpable, cannot be regarded as morally blameworthy. This holds true for all those we wish to deem monsters. No, Mr. Johan Kotze remains a child of God with the capacity to become a saint.

This piece shocked many. But the world is filled with heartless sinners and criminals of all sorts who have transformed themselves and their lives. In the Christian tradition, we often recall the story of the repentant criminal who was crucified beside Jesus. He was a man who had committed crimes punishable by death. Jesus promised him that, because of his repentance, "this day we will see each other in paradise." He was forgiven. The Bible is full of stories of reckless, immoral, and criminal people who transformed their lives, who became saints. Peter, the disciple who betrayed a friendship and denied Jesus—not once, but three times—

was forgiven and became the chief of the apostles. Paul, the violent persecutor of those faithful to the fledgling Christian faith, became the sower who planted Christian communities in the gentile world.

Let us condemn ghastly acts, but let us never relinquish the hope that the doers of the most heinous deeds can and may change. In many ways, that was the basis of our truth-and-reconciliation process. The stories we heard at the TRC were horrific, some were bloodcurdling, yet we witnessed extraordinary acts of forgiveness as perpetrator and victim embraced and did so publicly. We believed then, and I still believe now, that it is possible for people to change for the better. It is more than just possible; it is in our nature . . . in each and every one of us.

In my plea for the people of Modimolle to stop calling Mr. Kotze a monster, I called on my Christian faith for the examples needed. But the ability to separate the sin from the sinner is not a matter of faith or religion; neither is forgiveness. The Forgiveness Cycle is a universal and nonsectarian cycle. Obviously, in Mpho's faith and mine, our model of the ultimate example of forgiveness is Jesus Christ, who on the cross was able to ask for forgiveness for those who were torturing and ultimately killed him. But forgiveness does not require faith. For some people faith makes the process easier. But just as we do not forgive for others, we also do not forgive for God.

I have said before that given the same set of circumstances, under the same pressures and influences, I may have been a Hitler, or a Kotze. I would hope not. But I may have been. I will not label anyone beyond redemption, regardless of what that person has done. I have found that hope and goodness can sometimes emerge from even the unlikeliest of packages. As we have seen, forgiving does not condone an act. Forgiveness does not relieve someone of responsibility for what they have done. Forgiveness does not erase accountability. It is not about turning a blind eye or even turning the other cheek. It is not about letting someone off the hook or saying it is okay to do something monstrous. Forgiveness is simply about understanding that every one of us is both inherently good and inherently flawed. Within every hopeless situation and every seemingly hopeless person lies the possibility of transformation.

So when I am asked whether some people are beyond forgiveness, my answer is no. My heart has been broken a thousand times over at the cruelty and suffering I have seen human beings unjustly and mercilessly inflict upon one another. Yet still I know and believe that forgiveness is always called for, and reconciliation is always possible.

My words are not a magic eraser, able to wipe away the deep harm and suffering we may feel. True forgiveness is not superficial or glib. It is a deep and thorough look at the reality of a situation. It is an honest accounting of both actions and consequences. It is a conversation that is only done when it is done. It is a path as unique as the people who choose to walk it. My path may not be the same as yours. But the thing that makes us walk this path is the same. We all want to be free of the pain of living with a broken and unforgiving heart. We want to free ourselves of the corrosive emotions that threaten to burn away the love and joy residing in us. We want to heal our broken places. It would be wonderful if we lived in a world where there was no harm, no hurt, no violence, no cruelty. I have certainly not lived my life in such a world, but I do believe it to be possible. Surely he must be senile, you say. But these are not the fantastical beliefs of a man of advanced years. I know in my heart that peace is possible. I know it is possible in your life, and I know it is possible in mine. I know it is possible for our children, our grandchildren, and the generations that follow. But I also know that it is only possible if this peace begins with each of us. Peace is built with every small and large act of forgiveness.

We cannot walk the Fourfold Path in shame or silence. After all, the first step on the path is telling our stories. The process is not quiet, and it is not always pretty. It calls for a vulnerability that can be uncomfortable at best. It will ask much of you, sometimes more than you think you can give. However, the gifts and the freedom that will be returned to you are beyond measure.

We invite you to lay down your sorrows and trust that nothing will be asked of you that you are not able to give. Forgiving is always worthwhile in the end. To get to that end, we must make a beginning, a first step. The first step will be telling your truth. We begin by Telling the Story.

But first, let us pause to listen to what the heart hears.

You have stood at this junction before
You will stand at this junction again
And if you pause you can ask yourself
Which way to turn
You can turn away from your own sadness
And run the race named revenge
You will run that tired track again and again

Or you can admit your own pain
And walk the path that ends
In this direction lies freedom, my friend
I can show you where hope and wholeness make their homes
But you can't push past your anguish on your way there
To find the path to peace
You will have to meet your pain
And speak its name

Summary
Understanding the Fourfold Path

- Nothing is unforgivable.
- There is no one who is beyond redemption, and to deem someone a monster is to take away that person's accountability for his or her actions.
- We always have a choice whether to walk the Revenge Cycle or the Forgiveness Cycle.
- In the Revenge Cycle, we reject our pain and suffering and believe that by hurting the person who hurt us our pain will go away.
- In the Forgiveness Cycle, we face our pain and suffering and move toward acceptance and healing by walking the Fourfold Path.
- These are the steps of the Fourfold Path: Telling the Story, Naming the Hurt, Granting Forgiveness, and Renewing or Releasing the Relationship.

Meditation

Walking the Path

The following image is of a finger labyrinth, patterned after the walking labyrinth in the floor of Chartres Cathedral in France. A finger labyrinth is "walked" by tracing the path with a finger of the non-dominant hand. The advantage of a finger labyrinth is its accessibility. It can be carried with you and used almost anywhere at any time.

1. For this meditation you will set your intention to remain open to the forgiveness journey before you enter this labyrinth.
2. As you follow the labyrinth path, notice the places where you lose your way, where you pause, where you meet resistance. Can you name what has been evoked in you?
3. At the center of the labyrinth, pause and ask for a blessing.
4. Follow the path back out.
5. As you exit the labyrinth, pause to offer thanks for this time of reflection.

You can turn to this labyrinth whenever you need to collect your thoughts along the Fourfold Path.

Stone Ritual

Marking the Path

1. Take your stone and trace around it four times in your journal, creating four circles.
2. In each circle, write the name of each step of the Four-fold Path:
   a. Telling the Story
   b. Naming the Hurt
   c. Granting Forgiveness
   d. Renewing or Releasing the Relationship
3. Write around each circle what resistances you notice as you consider walking the Fourfold Path.
4. Write down anything that is holding you back.

Journal Exercise

1. What would be the best outcome you could imagine, if you were to forgive?
2. How would your life be different?
3. How would your relationships be different—both your relationship to the one who harmed you and your relationships with others?

Part Two

THE FOURFOLD
PATH

Chapter 4

Telling the Story

IT WAS HOT.

During the day, the Karoo—that vast expanse of semi-desert in the middle of South Africa—is an oven. When we opened the car windows, the air rushed in as if from a blow-dryer set on high. The car windows were open; it was an act of desperate hope. We were sticky with sweat. We were tired. The children had started the backseat bickering that seems to come with fatigue and heat. We had been driving for hours, having left our home in Alice in the Eastern Cape before dawn. The whole family—four young children, Leah, and I—had piled into a station wagon for our trek to Swaziland.

In the 1960s, South Africa was in the fierce grip of apartheid. It was the reason for our trek. When the Bantu Education system of inferior education for black children was instituted by the government, Leah and I left the teaching profession in protest. We vowed we would do all in our power to ensure our children were never subjected to the brain-washing that passed for education in South Africa. Instead, we enrolled the children in schools in neighboring Swaziland. Naomi started boarding school at the tender age of six. Because of our three-year sojourn in England while I studied theology, Trevor and Thandi were older when they started to board. Six times each year we made the three-thousand-mile drive from Alice in the Eastern Cape to my parents' home in Krugersdorp. After spending the night with them, we would drive five hours to Swaziland, drop off or pick up the children at their schools, and drive back to Krugersdorp to rest before the long drive home. There were no hotels or inns that would accommodate black guests at any price.

On that blistering day we were on our way to leave the children at school. It wasn't the happy, chatty journey we had after picking them up. On those drives homeward the children were full of fun and news and the exciting prospect of holiday. This was the drop-off drive, and the coming fare-wells cast a slight pall over the mood of the family. The heat added another dimension to our despair. Up ahead, I saw a "Walls Ice Cream" sign. Our spirits lifted. I could almost taste the delicious, cold, sweet relief as I pulled up outside the shop.

We all clambered out of the car. I pushed open the door to the small store, which doubled as the local take-away, or carryout.

The boy behind the register looked up. He jerked his thumb. "Kaffirs must go to the window."

I looked at the window in the wall from which the contents of the store were barely visible. No black man's feet allowed on the hallowed ground of this dinky store. The only black people allowed inside were black women on their knees to scrub and sweep.

The rage seared me. The sadness of the impending separation from our children, the fatigue and frustration from the long, hot drive, the irritation with the children bickering in the backseat, and now this! I slammed my way out of the shop.

"Get back in the car!" I told everyone. They scrambled back, confusion creasing their faces, back into the angry heat. I was furious, and like so many frustrated parents, my temper flared. Underneath my temper, however, was a bright and burning wound.

It was such a small incident. It was nothing earthshattering. No one had bled. No one had died. But even now, as I tell the story, I recall how deep and real the hurt felt. It was a stinging hurt heaped on all the other hurts that were commonplace in our daily lives under apartheid. We were so used to these incidents that, at the time, I didn't consciously know I had to forgive the boy behind the register.

Stories are not always told from start to finish. Sometimes we don't even know they are stories. We simply begin to assemble the pieces, to make sense out of our experiences. In the car, I wanted the children to understand what had just happened to us, but first I had to face my own feelings of hopelessness. Families must find shared stories of their experiences, or everyone is left to their private pain and each member of the family feels alone and isolated. This happens whenever there is a crisis or cruelty, and calls for meaning to be made.

I did not want my children to tell themselves the story of supposed inferiority and justified inequality that was the master narrative of those bygone days. Instead, I told them about dignity and how one can only be robbed of it if one hands it to a thief. This "teaching moment" was how I also came to terms with what had just happened to my family. Later that night, when we had dropped off the children at school and Leah and I were alone, I discussed it with Leah. She had been there and knew what had happened, but in our shared words we again retold the story, and in doing so began to accept the facts of what had happened.

We all experience pain. This is the inescapable part of being human. Hurt, insult, harm, and loss are inevitable aspects of our lives. Psychology calls it "trauma," and it often leaves deep scars on our souls. However, it is not the trauma itself that defines us. It is the meaning we make of our experiences that defines both who we are and who we ultimately become. Walking away from the shop, even in anger, I was refusing to accept the valuation of myself as a second-class citizen undeserving of respect.

Every day we are faced with a possibility of being hurt by others; it is part and parcel of living and loving and being a member of the human family. Whether the harm is intentional or unintentional, the hurt is real. We may find ourselves the target of lies, betrayal, gossip, or even physical assault. Someone we love may reject us. Someone we trust may cheat us. Someone we consider a friend or someone we recognize as a stranger may insult us. Or we may find ourselves in the wrong place at the wrong time and fall victim to random violence or a tragic accident. Loved ones may be hurt or even killed. In any given moment we may be harmed profoundly. It is not fair. It is not deserved.

And yet it happens.

It is what we do next that matters most. Each time we are injured, we stand at the same fork in the road and choose to travel either the path of forgiveness or the path of retaliation. Even in the midst of righteous anger or rage, even if we are blinded by grief and pain, even if our suffering feels so immense and so unfair, we always make a choice. We can lash out in retaliation, demanding an eye for an eye in the false belief that, somehow, this will undo the initial harm or provide balm for our wounds. Or we can step toward the place of acceptance. We can recognize that we must give up all belief that we can change the past. The journey to acceptance begins in pain and ends in hope.

If you are reading this book, you have made this choice and are already on your journey. What is it you need to forgive? What happened to cause your pain? How have you been hurt? Whatever it may be, whatever has been broken or lost, can only be repaired and found again by telling the story of what happened.

Why Tell the Story

Telling the story is how we get our dignity back after we have been harmed. It is how we begin to take back what was taken from us, and how we begin to understand and make meaning out of our hurting.

Neuroscientists tell us that we have two kinds of memories, explicit and implicit. When we remember an event and know what happened, we form *explicit* memories—we know explicitly that we are remembering something. That's what most of us think memory is. But there is another kind. When we experience an event we are not consciously aware of, we form *implicit* memories. In other words, we don't realize we are remembering something. When Mpho's daughter Nyaniso was four she was attacked by a pair of Dobermans; the dogs were too big for their owner to control. For years, Nyaniso flinched whenever a dog approached. She didn't have the explicit memory of being terrorized; she had an implicit memory that caused a reaction in her. It was only years later, in the course of sharing family stories, that Nyaniso was able to transform her implicit memory into an explicit memory. She was able to integrate her memories through the act of telling her story. This was an important part of how she began to heal from the trauma. This is so for all of us. Telling our stories helps us integrate our implicit memories and begin to heal from our traumas.

Knowing our stories and histories is vital for us at any age. Marshall Duke, a psychologist from Emory University, began exploring resilience in children during the 1990s. He and a colleague developed a twenty-question survey called "Do You Know," which they gave to children to find out the stories children knew about their families. It turned out that the more children knew the stories of their families' history—the good, the bad, and the ugly—the more resilient the children turned out to be. Knowing their families' stories turned out to be "the best single predictor of children's emotional health and happiness." It also turned out that in following up on these children after the September 11, 2001, terrorist act in New York City, the children who scored high on the scale, who best knew their families' history—successes and failures—were most resilient in times of trauma or stress.[8] These children were connected to a larger story about their lives, to a bigger picture and context of who they were.

Just as this scale predicted the future health and happiness of the children in this study, so does knowing and telling our own stories of harm predict our future health and happiness in recovering from that trauma. When we know our stories and make sense of what has happened, we get connected to the larger story of our lives and its meaning. We become more resilient, we are able to handle stress, and we heal. Neuropsychiatrist Dan Siegel explains that the best predictor of how well a child will be attached to his or her parents—have positive, loving relationships—is whether the parents have a clear and coherent story about their lives and the traumas they have experienced. In other words, if you are able to talk about your life and the joys and sorrows you have experienced—if you know your story—you are much more likely to be a skillful parent. Your unhealed, unforgiven traumas will not rear their ugly heads, as our disowned experiences so often do. If we cannot seek forgiveness and healing for our own benefit, perhaps we can seek it for the sake of our children.

But how do we do this? How do we tell the story?

Tell the Truth

The Truth and Reconciliation Commission was first and foremost a truth commission. There could be no reconciliation between South Africa's past and South Africa's future without the truth. It is the same for you and me. The truth prevents us from pretending that the things that happened did not happen. How we begin is by first letting the truth be heard in all its rawness, in all its ugliness, and in all its messiness. This is what we did in South Africa, this is what I did after that long-ago day in the Karoo, and this is what you must do for what has happened to you.

Start with the Facts

Telling the facts of your story is the most important element of this first step, and it is how you begin to take back what was taken from you. When you tell your story, it is as if you are putting the puzzle pieces back together again, one hesitant memory at a time. In the beginning, your memories and your facts, depending on what the trauma is and when it happened, may be fragmented and hard to articulate. They may not follow a chronological order or be told in a linear fashion. All of this is understandable. This is how it is for Mpho when she recalls the day of Angela's murder:

Last week was the anniversary of Angela's death. We went through the day, the girls and I, feeling out of sorts and not recognizing what was going on. At the end of the day we realized what it was that had been churning in us, that it was the anniversary of her death, and we felt this profound and renewed sadness. Nyaniso had a particularly hard time with Angela's death. Angela was found in her room, but what she told me last week was that they had argued that morning.

It was a silly argument over whether or not she had a school uniform to wear, but they had parted in sort of a bad space. I didn't know this for a whole year. It was the first time I was hearing it. Even a year later we are still filling in holes in the story. There may be some pieces that we never know, like what exactly happened on that day. All I know is that so much was lost.

It was a usual morning, with me sort of flying about the house trying to pack and get the kids off to school. Angela always seemed to be a half step ahead of me. Angela knew how to handle Onalenna's morning crankies and usher her into the day in a really sweet way, which is not a skill I have. For some reason that morning I remember I had done my makeup in the kitchen and had charged out the door in a big rush. Usually Angela would come rushing out after me, wanting to know what to make for dinner, but I don't think she did that morning. In the first few months of working for us, I would go over step-by-step how to cook a meal, but now she had it down and I could just give her the menu and she would know what to do.

That day, for some reason, I had come back to the house after dropping the girls off. Angela was in the kitchen doing dishes when I got there. She didn't say anything or indicate there was anything wrong, but I do remember she had an odd look on her face. I asked her if everything was okay and she said yes.

Onalenna had a swim class and I had to be in town that afternoon, so I asked my brother-in-law, Mthunzi, to pick up Onalenna and drop her off at home after school, where she could stay with Angela until it was time for swim class.

When Mthunzi got to the house, he called me and said there was no answer from the house. We have a security gate that is operated from inside the house. I remember feeling a bit annoyed, a bit huffy. Angela knew the girls could be dropped off any time after two o'clock, and she was always there and always called me if she was going to be away from the house for more than five minutes. It was weird and it didn't seem right. I tried to call the house. I tried to call her mobile phone. It was very unusual. I told Mthunzi to bring Onalenna to my office instead. I called the house over and over again throughout the afternoon. I kept calling and calling. No answer. I thought it was really strange and very unlike her to be so unreachable. I asked my mom to drive Onalenna to swim class, so on my way to my mom's house to drop Onalenna off, I decided to stop by my house and see what had happened. Things seemed off. The garage door wouldn't open. The back gate was open in a way it never was. I backed out of the driveway and drove to my mom's to drop my daughter off. I knew that whatever I might find in the house I didn't want to find it with Onalenna next to me.

I called Mthunzi and told him, "There is something that doesn't feel right at the house." I asked him to meet me there. We arrived back at the house at the same time and went in through the front door. Once inside the house, I knew immediately that something was wrong. I went to Angela's room and the bed was unmade, which was very unusual for this time of day. We started walking back toward the bedrooms. I walked past my room and saw the basket of makeup I had left in the kitchen that morning on top of my bed. It seems such a small matter, but that's when I really knew something was horribly wrong. Angela was very particular and would never put something on top of a bed she had already made up, and certainly not my makeup basket, which was full of powders that could mess up the bedcovers. We then turned down the hallway, and I noticed it was unusually dark and that Nyaniso's bedroom door was closed. Once she had finished cleaning, which she would have done by this late in the day, Angela always left the bedroom doors open. I told Mthunzi this is not right. He opened the door to Nyaniso's room and that's when I saw her.

She was on the floor.

There was so much blood.

I asked him to check if she had a pulse. He said he didn't think so.

At that point the neighborhood crime watch arrived and told us we needed to leave. Our home was now a crime scene. I didn't know it at the time, but we would never be able to call it home again.

Mpho's memories of the event are clear and explicit. The small and seemingly unrelated details come back to her as she remembers her makeup basket, the look on Angela's face when she came back to the house, the certain knowledge that afternoon that something was wrong, and her instinct to shield Onalenna from whatever it might be. There is so much more to her story than the facts, but she must get the facts out first. Even the small details can be important. They are threads by which we make sense of what has happened. Just tell the story as you remember it.

The Cost of Not Telling

Even if intellectually I know that it is through my storytelling I will begin to heal from trauma, it is not always easy emotionally to take the first step. It can be a risky endeavor. There is the risk of being hurt again, of not being believed, of not being affirmed. But when we lock our stories inside us, the initial injury is often compounded. If I tuck my secrets and my stories away in shame or fear or silence, then I am bound to my victimhood and my trauma. If Mpho had never told the story of what happened on that day, she would have remained at the mercy of that tragic experience.

It is not always easy to tell your story, but it is the first critical step on the path to freedom and forgiveness. We saw this so palpably in the TRC, when the victims of apartheid were able to come forward to tell their stories. They were relieved to have a place of safety and affirmation in which to share their experiences. They were also relieved of the ongoing victimization they suffered from believing that no one would ever truly know what they had endured or believe the stories they had to tell. When you tell your story, you no longer have to carry your burden alone.

A young man, whom we will call Jeffrey, just celebrated his thirtieth birthday but has carried an untold story from when he was twelve. He is a large, imposing man with a deep voice. Yet when he speaks of what happened almost two decades earlier, he sounds like a small boy again—sad, lost, and alone. A teacher and coach—a man Jeffrey's single mother had trusted to be a mentor and role model for her adolescent son—sexually molested Jeffrey at an after-school sporting event. Jeffrey never told his mother or anyone, afraid of bringing shame to his family, afraid of hurting his mother, afraid he had somehow done something wrong and caused this teacher to do what he had done. Unable to speak of it, Jeffrey became an angry, sullen teenager who didn't trust anyone, especially adults. He dropped out of his after-school activities and avoided the teacher as much as possible. When they did run into each other, the man acted as if nothing had happened, which made Jeffrey question his own sanity. Jeffrey describes his life in terms of "before" and "after." Before it happened, he had been a happy boy, confident, excited about the future and who he might become. After the incident, the world seemed bleak and unsafe. It wasn't until Jeffrey met a woman and fell in love that he dared share the story of what had happened to him. The woman, whom he would later marry, encouraged him to forgive his teacher. She told Jeffrey that by not forgiving he had let this man continue to abuse him for almost two decades.

For Jeffrey, it took many years to find someone he felt safe with enough to tell his story: "I wasted so much of my life living in shame and guilt, feeling like I had done something wrong. When I told Eliza [not her real name] what had happened, I was so afraid she would look at me differently, that she would reject me and no longer love me. It was the thinking of a twelve-year-old boy, not a thirty-year-old man." Trauma like Jeffrey's can cause us to stay trapped in the painful times of our lives and limit ourselves in countless ways. The path of forgiveness leads back to where we were trapped, so we can rescue the parts of ourselves we have given up. Through sharing his story with his wife, Jeffrey was able to go back, with her support, and free that twelve-year-old boy who had done nothing wrong.

Once Jeffrey was able to tell the story, he said it was as if a weight was lifted off his chest. He felt as if he could take a deep breath for the first time in years. Jeffrey continued to tell his story, first to his mother and then, eventually, to other men who had also suffered in silence and shame after being sexually abused. "It wasn't as if everything was made okay by telling my secret, and I lived happily ever after," he says. "But it was as though I had been locked in a dungeon for years, only to discover that I had the key to get out all along. I was hard on myself about that as well and regretful of all the years I had wasted. Once I joined a group of other survivors and heard their stories and shared mine, it was somehow better. Each time I talked, it was easier. I was able to help other men who had similar experiences, and the more compassion I had for what they had experienced, the more compassion I had for my own twelve-year-old self. It's hard to explain, but eventually I came to a place where I was okay with what happened because it gave me this empathy and ability to help people that I may never have had otherwise."

As we will see and discuss in later chapters, this acceptance and recognition of the hidden gifts that suffering can bring is an important part of healing and forgiveness.

Deciding Whom to Tell

One of the most important decisions you will make is choosing whom to tell your story. Ideally, as we were able to do with the TRC, you can tell your story to the person who caused you harm. There is a profound reclaiming of dignity and strength when you are able to stand in front of your abuser, stand in your truth, and speak of how that person hurt you. I believe this is the quickest way to find both peace and the will to forgive. It is not, however, always possible or even practical. To work, the perpetrator has to be receptive, and you have to be sure they will not cause you more harm. Ideally, they have shown remorse, are asking for your forgiveness, and are willing to witness the pain they have caused by listening to your story. In the TRC, we did not allow any cross-examination or questioning of the story being told. Each individual was able to share their pain, loss, anger, grief, trauma, from a place of safety and complete affirmation. Many victims had questions about how their loved ones had died, and they needed these questions answered in order to move on and heal. This is how it was for Angela's family and how it is for many who lose loved ones from an act of violence. They needed to know the facts before they could accept what had happened. Some needed to know exactly how their loved ones were killed, whether they suffered, and why the perpetrators had done what they had done. Only when the questions of the past had been answered, could they move on to the future. Mpho has told me she will never forget the shriek of anguished despair that came from Angela's sister and mother when she had to tell them that Angela was dead. They had many questions, some of which Mpho could answer, and some of which she could not.

In the ideal model of forgiveness, there is an exchange of stories, and if done with total honesty and no justification or rationalization on the part of the perpetrator, there can be great understanding and healing between the two people.

Even if you are able to speak directly to the one you want to forgive, it may be better for you to share your story with others first, whether that is a close family member or a friend. You may also turn to your religious leader, to your therapist, or directly to God. As long as the one to whom you tell the story is affirming, empathetic, and trustworthy, you will move forward in the process of forgiving and benefit from this step in the Fourfold Path.

Whether you tell your story to the person who harmed you or to a surrogate, the important element of this first step is simply to tell the story, to acknowledge the harm that happened. If there is no one you trust, then you can always write your story down in a letter to the person who harmed you, even if it is a letter you cannot send. When we tell the truth about our hurt and our loss, we lessen the power it has over us.

How to Listen

- Do not question the facts.
- Do not cross-examine.
- Create a safe space.
- Acknowledge what happened.
- Empathize with the pain.

It is important to state that telling the story is not a single action, nor is it a finite event. It is an ongoing process within the unfolding process of forgiving and healing. The story Mpho told in the days immediately after Angela's murder is not the exact same story she told a year later. Our stories evolve as our understanding evolves, as our acceptance evolves, and as our meaning-making evolves. The more you understand your own story, and the further you have progressed through the steps along the Fourfold Path, the more likely it is you will be able to meet the perpetrator in a way that will contribute to your healing and the renewing, or releasing, of the relationship.

Telling the Story Directly to the Perpetrator

If you do choose to speak to the person who has harmed you, be aware that it is a delicate matter. If not done carefully, it may make matters worse. We have very little understanding of forgiveness and few rituals for forgiving in modern society. It is easy for people to feel attacked or become defensive when confronted. The power of the human mind to justify its actions is truly endless. No villain has ever thought he was a villain. Hitler, Stalin, every terrorist and serial murderer—every person has a reason why his or her actions were justified. The purse snatcher who clobbers the old lady over the head could not move his arm if he did not think—at least in that moment—that what he was doing was the right thing. The way to understand any enemy is to realize that, from his perspective, he is not a villain but a hero.

There is no guarantee the person who harmed you will acknowledge that what they did was wrong, yet there are ways to increase the likelihood that telling the story will lead to resolution rather than more conflict. If it is possible, you can begin by affirming your relationship with this person and its importance to you. What has this person meant to you? How have they helped you, not just harmed you? Our relationships are rarely one-dimensional, especially with intimates. My father, who could be boorish and abusive, could also be funny, engaging, and kind. If you can show the person that you see their goodness, then they don't have to work so hard to defend it.

If you can, have empathy for why the perpetrator may have done what they did. Empathy is a social contagion. If you have empathy for the one who victimized you, it is much more likely that they will have empathy for you. This is not guaranteed to work, but it can help. We often see people as independent and acting solely on their free will, but the truth is we are interdependent. We are embedded in social webs that affect our choices and our behavior. In South Africa, we saw how the political environment contributed not only to political violence but also to

Note

If you are ready to speak directly to the person who harmed you and it is not possible, practical, or safe to tell your story in person, you can write them a letter. You can write a letter telling your story, even if you will never send it or are unable to send it. The healing will still happen.

social, and even domestic, violence. As a mother, Mpho is keenly aware of the power of peer pressure on her teenage daughter. Sometimes the teenager's better choices have been molded by her friends' attitudes and opinions. Sometimes the influence has been less benign but no less deniable. No person is an island, and if we see the ways we are connected, we can understand another's actions with much more compassion.

Telling the Story Publicly

"At first we didn't feel like talking," says Lynn Wagner. "It was as if we were stumbling around in the dark, wondering who turned off the lights and what we were going to bang into next. Sometimes we would feel like yelling and screaming, but there was nobody to yell and scream at. One minute they were with us, and the next minute they were gone. We didn't get to say good-bye to them."

Lynn Wagner and her husband, Dan, lost their two teenage daughters when the car they were driving was hit by a drunk driver. They now share their story in churches, at universities, and with groups of offenders in their local jail. Before they could tell their story publicly, however, they first told it to their family and friends, as Dan Wagner relates it here:

> Lynn and I and our two teenage girls, Mandie and Carrie, attended the Saturday evangelical event, along with about twenty thousand other people. Lynn had gone earlier that day to the prayer meeting, and the girls and I caught up with her in the afternoon.
>
> We left Beachfest that evening and headed for our car parked in a quiet neighborhood near the beach. It was where we always parked when we would go to the beach boardwalk. We drove up Cayuga Street toward Broadway, heading home to the Live Oak area. A woman, who was drunk and had cocaine and methamphetamine in her system, had just picked up her two children from a babysitter and was driving her Suburban on Windsor Street toward Cayuga at almost fifty miles per hour. She ran the stop sign and crashed into us on the left side of our minivan. The

impact sent us into a power pole and then onto a neighbor's front yard.

Neither Lynn nor I have any memories of the accident and very few memories of that day. We woke up in Dominican Hospital, Lynn on Sunday morning and me on Monday morning. Lynn had three fractured ribs and a broken pelvis in two places that prevented her from putting any weight on one leg for about six weeks. I had no fractures but suffered torn cartilage in my chest, a sprained coccyx, a neck injury, and embedded safety glass in my face and elbow that had to be removed later. Both of us had concussions.

My pastor has said that he told me right away when I seemed coherent. I don't remember. The first time I remember grasping it was when someone visiting me in my hospital room had said that they were sorry for my loss. I had asked, "What loss?" They told me I had lost my girls. I remember sharing that news with others who came to visit as if it were a baseball score; it's amazing what shock can do to your emotions.

My mom and dad in Oregon were called the night of the accident and drove down right away. They had a key to our house and let themselves in, and then came to the hospital. I remember how comforting it was to see them when my bed was wheeled into Lynn's room. My dad told me the first thing he did when he saw me was reach for my legs to see if they were still there.

I was discharged to go home on Thursday, but Lynn was sent to the recovery care unit, located in the former Santa Cruz Community Hospital building. It was the hospital where both Mandie and Carrie were born.

After telling their story to the people closest to them, Dan and Lynn decided that, to heal, they needed to tell Lisa, the woman who had crashed into them. They also decided that to continue on in life, with any future joy or peace, they had to find a way to forgive Lisa. They began to write to her while she was in prison, and she wrote back. Today, when they tell their story publicly, their story includes Lisa's story. In fact, Lisa, now out of prison, goes with Dan and Lynn when they speak to groups. The three of them tell their story together. If it is hard to imagine a forgiveness that allows you to be in a relationship with the person responsible for your children's deaths, this is understandable. It wasn't easy and it wasn't quick, but that is the miracle of forgiveness.

Do not worry too much about how or where you tell your story. What is most important to healing is that you tell your story. You may find that your story changes as time goes on, as you move through the forgiving process. It will change as you come to a deeper understanding of the hurt you experienced and of those who hurt you. Some have made the choice to tell their stories publicly, and they find a unique comfort in doing so. We saw this to be true in the TRC, and we see it across the world in public forums and websites where people

Forgiveness Story Websites

www.theforgivenessproject.com
www.forgivenessfoundation.org
www.projectforgive.com

share their stories of loss, forgiveness, and reconciliation. It can be powerfully healing to read about how others travel the difficult road of forgiveness.

We may need to tell our stories many times over, to many different people, and in many different forms before we are ready to move forward in the forgiveness process. We also may find that just telling our stories relieves a burden we have carried. When we tell our stories, we are practicing a form of acceptance. When we tell our stories, we are saying, "This horrible thing has happened. I cannot go back and change it, but I can refuse to stay trapped in the past forever." We have reached acceptance when we finally recognize that paying back someone in kind will never make us feel better or undo what has been done. To quote the comedian Lily Tomlin, "Forgiveness means giving up all hope for a better past."

Mpho has chosen to share her story of Angela's murder and her journey along the Fourfold Path of forgiveness. It is not a journey that is easy for any of us, and telling the story is just the beginning. We must then go beyond the facts of what happened to the feelings of how we were hurt. It is important to tell your story. It is equally important not to get trapped in your story. It is not just what happened to us that matters but how what happened hurt us. In the next chapter, we will find ways to name that hurt.

But first, let us pause to listen to what the heart hears.

To whom shall I tell my story?
Who will hear my truth
Who can open the space that my words want to fill
Who will hold open the space for the words that tumble out
in fast cutting shards
And the words that stumble hesitantly into the world
unsure of their welcome

Can you hold that space open for me?
Can you keep your questions and suggestions and judgments at bay
Can you wait with me for the truths that stay hidden behind my
sadness, my fear, my forgetting, and my pain
Can you just hold open a space for me to tell my story

Summary

Telling the Story

- Speak the truth.
- Start with the facts.
- Tell your story first to a friend, loved one, or trusted person.
- Consider telling the story to the person who harmed you, or writing a letter.
- Accept that whatever has happened cannot be changed or undone.

Meditation

The Box of Sorrows

You may choose to gather about you the cloak of safety you created in chapter 2.

1. *Create a safe space.* Bring to mind a place of safety. It can be real or imaginary. See this place fully and inhabit it. Are you indoors or outdoors? Is it a large, open space or a cozy place? What does it smell like? What does the air feel like on your skin? What sounds do you hear? Music? A crackling fire? Birdsong? A babbling brook or a fountain? Ocean waves? The hushed whisper of grass swaying in a breeze? There is an inviting place to sit comfortably. Relax into this place. It is your place of safety.

2. *Someone is calling for you.* The one who is calling for you speaks in a voice filled with warmth, love, and delight. When you are ready, welcome this person into your safe place. Notice how the person's presence increases your sense of safety and assurance. Who is your companion? Is it a loved one, a friend, or a spiritual figure? Is it someone who is accepting, affirming, and utterly trustworthy?

3. *Between you and your companion sits an open box.* Look at the box. It is small and light enough for you to lift and hold. Notice its size, shape, and texture. What is unique about this box? Tell your companion the story of the hurt you carry. Tell the truth about how you

have been wounded, disdained, disrespected, shamed, or disregarded in as much detail as you can remember. As you speak, see the hurt and the words pouring out of you like a stream. Watch the stream being poured into the open box. Speak until you have finished. Your companion has time to listen. All your companion wants in this moment is to be with you until you are done. When you have said all there is to say, close the box of sorrows.

4. *Take the box into your lap.* You may want to sit with it in your lap for a few moments. When you are ready, hand the box to your trusted companion. Know that your box is in safe hands. You do not need to carry those sorrows any longer.

5. *When you are ready, you may leave your place of safety.* Know that your trusted companion will take your box of sorrows from that place but will return it should you ever have need.

Stone Ritual

Whispering to the Stone

1. Now that you have imagined yourself telling your story into your box of sorrows, it is time to actually give voice to what happened. There is power in words that are spoken.
2. Pick up your stone and tell the story of what happened in as much detail as you can. Remember to speak the truth, as much of it as you can remember. Speaking to the stone can be an emotionally safe way to prepare for speaking your story to another person.

Journal Exercise

1. Open your journal and write your story. Fill as many pages as you need.
2. Writing is a very powerful way to tell your story. As you write, you may remember details you did not recall when you were speaking.
3. If you feel safer or more comfortable, you can always read what you have written to a person you love and trust.
4. Later you may choose to read or send what you have written to the perpetrator, but we encourage you to first continue along the Fourfold Path. The story is only the beginning.

Chapter 5

Naming the Hurt

"WHAT KIND OF A MOTHER AM I that my child can be so hurt? Not once but twice. I am so angry. I feel so inadequate, so humiliated, so ashamed." The words and the feelings poured forth from the woman in a torrent as Mpho listened.

Mpho had been called to the hospital by the gynecologist on duty. It was the second time in less than a year that the doctor was seeing the woman's eight-year-old daughter. The last time, though she showed signs of sexual molestation, the child's story had not added up. The court's prosecutor had refused to press forward with a case against the man the child had accused.

This time was different. This time the mother had found her daughter's bloodstained underwear. She had taken the girl to the police station and then to the hospital. They had ridden in a police van to the child's neighborhood and, from the safety of the police car, the girl had pointed out the neighbor who had molested and terrorized her: "If you tell, I will kill your mommy and your daddy and your sister and your baby brother," he had said to her. This time the child was given assurances that no one would die and that the scary man would be taken away. She didn't need to make up a perpetrator. She told the truth. And told it again, and again, and again—to her mother, then to the police, then to the doctor.

As the little girl told her story, unpacked her feelings, and named her hurt and fear, her mother had listened in anguished silence. By the time Mpho was called to the hospital, the little girl had repeated her story several times over. Frankly, she was sick of it.

Mpho arrived at the hospital feeling a little harried. She hadn't found someone to stay with her (then) five-year-old daughter Nyaniso. She had done the mommy thing, packing snacks and distractions for her daughter in order to take her along for the pastoral call.

The little girl was small for her age. She and the tall-for-her-age Nyaniso were similar in size. For once the absence of childcare was a godsend. The little girl was sick of telling her story. She just wanted to be done with it and get to the important business of playing. Nyaniso filled the role of playmate perfectly. With the children occupied, the mothers could talk.

The little girl's mother had suffering written all over her face as she told the story. Now, in a gush of anguished words she needed to name her hurt.

Every one of us has a story to tell of when we were hurt. Once we are done telling our stories—the technical details of who, when, where, and what was done to us—we must name the hurt. Giving the emotion a name is the way we come to understand how what happened affected us. After we've told the facts of what happened, we must face our feelings. We are each hurt in our own unique ways, and when we give voice to this pain, we begin to heal it.

As we begin to heal, our relationship to the story loosens and we can choose when and where to share it. Until the healing begins, we may find ourselves stuck, rigidly repeating our story—or pieces of our story—to anyone and everyone, irrespective of the person or the situation. Many of us have seen people who mutter their story aloud to themselves over and over. They are stuck in their trauma, literally driven crazy by their inability to transcend what has happened to them. Healing memory requires the careful assembly of the puzzle pieces of experience, but once we know what has happened, we must move beyond the bare facts to the raw feelings. While we may be reluctant to face the truth of our feelings or the depth of our pain, it is the only way to heal and move forward. My dear friend, Father Michael Lapsley, was the victim of a letter bomb during apartheid, which robbed him of both his hands and his sight in one eye. Father Lapsley has devoted his life to teaching people how to heal through storytelling. From his own experience, he is keenly aware of the need for forgiveness in response to trauma. He reminds us of the importance of confronting and soothing the raw reality of our emotions. In his words, "We can't let go of feelings that we don't own."

We give voice to our hurts not to be victims or martyrs, but to find freedom from the resentment, anger, shame, or self-loathing that can fester and build inside us when we do not touch our pain and learn to forgive.

Why Must We Name the Harm?

Often it can seem easier or safer to simply dismiss a hurt, stuff it down, push it away, pretend it didn't happen, or rationalize it, telling ourselves we really shouldn't feel the way we do. But a hurt is a hurt. A loss is a loss. And a harm felt but denied will always find a way to express itself. When I bury my hurt in shame or silence, it begins to fester from the inside out. I feel the pain more acutely, and I suffer even more because of it. Divorce court dockets tell this story with miserable frequency. Marriages crumble under the weight of unspoken resentments and unacknowledged hurts. When we ignore the pain, it grows bigger and bigger, and like an abscess that is never drained, eventually it will rupture. When that happens, it can reach into every area of our lives—our health, our families, our jobs, our friendships, our faith, and our very ability to feel joy may be diminished by the fallout from resentments, anger, and hurts that are never named.

We must each be especially courageous and name the hurts that cause us to feel shame or diminish us. When our dignity is violated, it serves no one if we stuff the injury away in the closet of our disowned past. We do not need to succumb to the temptation to meet such a violation with retaliation. The only way to heal this hurt is to give voice to what ails us. It is only in this way that we can keep our pain and loss from taking root inside us. It is only in this way that we have a chance for freedom.

We must do everything possible to dig the hurt out at the very roots that have bound us to it for so long. And the only way to reach the taproot is with the truth. It has often been said that we are as sick as the secrets we keep. Often the initial harm done to us is compounded by our own shame and silence about what we have suffered. This can be especially true for survivors of rape, incest, and other kinds of sexual abuse. Women around the world are told it is their fault they were assaulted or raped. Sometimes children are forced to keep the secrets of adults. The little girl whose story opened this chapter was one such child. She could have grown up believing that somehow she was responsible for or deserving of the violation and maltreatment she endured. Mercifully, her experience was different. As children we may not be able to name the harms we experience, but as adults we must give name to any abuse that still lives within us. We are not responsible for what breaks us, but we can be responsible for what puts us back together again. Naming the hurt is how we begin to repair our broken parts.

When Is It Necessary to Name the Hurt?

You may ask yourself, how do I know when a hurt needs to be voiced? How do I know when an injury must be named rather than shrugged off? Won't it be a full-time job if I must have a forgiveness process for every time someone insults or slights me, or every occasion on which I find my pride wounded? The truth is we engage a process whenever there

is an injury or violation. Sometimes we traverse the cycle
of forgiveness so rapidly we barely notice our feet touching
the steps. When my two-year-old at play knocks over my
favorite vase, I might swing around and smack her hand, a
useless act of retaliation masquerading as discipline. Instead,
I could say, "Oh, no! I loved that vase. It was a birthday gift
from my best friend. I'm so sad. We should play that game
outside. Oh, well, let's sweep up the mess." Though I wasn't
paying attention, all the steps were there. I stood at the fork
in the road and chose the way of forgiveness. I told the story,
I named the hurt, and I acknowledged that my two-year-old
was a human toddler with much to learn. And I accepted that
the broken vase could not be unbroken. Just that quickly it
was done and I could renew the relationship of a loving parent with an active child.

So how do we know when we need to walk the cycle of
forgiveness more slowly or deliberately? There are no hard-
and-fast rules. We cannot categorize all the different types
of hurt and tell you what will take time and what will not.
Each of us is different, and each of us will approach harm
differently depending on our circumstances. The single most
important thing is to share our sorrows, pains, fears, and
grief.

My younger sister called me a crybaby. Though the insult
was probably warranted, it still stung. "What other people
think of you is none of your business" was my mother's
assessment. She meant that my sister's words shouldn't matter
to me, and I should just ignore her unkind opinion. While
this may be true, and ideally we all could let the negative
judgments of others just roll off our backs, we still find that

the opinions of others can hurt and hurt deeply. A physical wound is sometimes the easiest to name, forgive, and heal from because it is obvious and tangible. A psychological wound is harder to name. It can attack our sense of safety, our need for acceptance and belonging, our identity, and our sense of worth as a human being. This is what the girl's mother expressed in the hospital—her identity and her sense of worth as a mother had been violated. Humiliation can cut just as deeply as the sharpest of blades. We can call out for help when someone is attacking us physically, but what aid do we need when the attack is emotional, when we feel ignored or rejected or slighted?

In her book *Dignity,* Donna Hicks explains that the pain felt from everyday assaults on our dignity are not imaginary. They can undermine our self-worth and our relationships with others. She also points out that neuroscientists have shown that a psychological wound, such as being excluded, stimulates the same part of the brain that is stimulated when there is a physical wound. In other words, our brains process and feel these injuries in the same way. They do not distinguish one type of hurt from another. That research dispels the old children's rhyme that "sticks and stones may break my bones but words will never hurt me." In actual fact, words do hurt us. They cut us to the quick. Whether pain is felt physically or emotionally, we face the same set of questions about how we will respond or react. If you hit me, do I hit you back? If you call me a name, do I find an even stronger invective to hurl back at you? If you dehumanize me, do I find a way to diminish your dignity or find someone else to oppress to make myself feel better? The never-ending cycle of revenge and retaliation, of hurt begetting hurt, of payback and vengeance, can be physical, verbal, or emotional.

Never Naming the Hurt

Never naming the hurt can have unimagined and unimaginable consequences in our lives. While away at university, a woman we'll call Clara Walsh received a phone call that would change her life. Her older sister, Kim, had been killed in a car accident. The police believed Kim was given a date-rape drug at a local bar and then was driven away in a car full of strangers, a group of men. The car they were in was traveling at sixty miles per hour when it crashed into a cement pillar. Everyone was killed instantly. Clara recalled:

> I didn't know what it meant to have someone die. One second they are there, and the next they are gone. I was scared, shocked, and so angry. I had no answers to any of my questions because the men in the car with my sister also died. I flew home for the funeral, but nobody in my family would talk about what had happened. She was my only sister, and it was as if there had been some agreement that my sister would never be mentioned again. I was confused, only nineteen years old, and so lost. Nobody cried together. Nobody spoke about the accident. Nobody told me how to act when somebody I loved died. I had no frame of reference. There was no model for grieving or healing.
>
> I went back to college and had horrible nightmares about my sister's death, her body mutilated, strangers hurting her. I didn't know how to ask for help. I didn't even know I needed help. Eventually, my jaw completely locked

up from clenching my teeth so hard. I had to have surgery to open it up again. I continued on in school and eventually got married and had children. For ten years I was so afraid that if I loved someone they would die. Horrible scenarios played out in my head whenever my husband went off to work, whenever one of my children was out of my sight. I was so sure they would never come back.

It was as if the world became a dangerous place when my sister died. I lost so many years of my life living in fear, unable to talk about my sister's death, not knowing how to express what I felt and not knowing that I needed to grieve. I shut down and eventually my marriage ended. I was so depressed, but I learned to pretend everything was okay when it wasn't. Eventually I started drinking to numb the pain and numb the fear. I began to self-destruct, turning to drugs and alcohol to cope with life, cope with my feelings, and cope with all the fear. Sometimes I wonder what it would be like to go back in time to my sister's funeral and do it all over again. My life would have turned out so differently. My children's lives would have turned out so differently. If I could have named the hurt, talked about my fears, shared my feelings, it would have changed everything.

The Role of Grief

When we experience any type of loss that causes us pain or suffering, there is always grief. While much has been written about grief, it is mostly directed at those who have lost a loved one. Grief does not only occur when someone dies. Grief happens whenever we lose something that is precious to us, even our trust, our faith, or our innocence. It is important to understand the role grief plays in the forgiveness process and specifically within this step of Naming the Hurt.

Grief is how we both cope with and release the pain we feel. Grief has many well-documented stages—denial, anger, bargaining, depression, and ultimately acceptance. Just as we experience these after the trauma of a loved one's death, we often experience the same stages during and after any other major trauma, such as a betrayal or an assault. We may cycle through the stages of grief or jump from one stage to another and back again. There is no fixed time, no fixed order, no one way of experiencing the grief associated with a loss. One may be in denial and then find oneself in depression, or one may be in acceptance and then find oneself in anger again. There is no right way to grieve, but grieving itself is essential. Grief is how we come to terms not only with the hardship we have endured, but also with what could have been if life had taken a different course. We grieve as much for what might have been as for what was.

When we name our hurts, we have moved out of the stage of denial. We cannot honestly name our feelings and be in denial at the same time. But we must not berate ourselves even for our denial. It exists for a reason. Denial protects us from remembered pain and can serve to pace our grief. When a loss feels unbearable or overwhelming, denial can be a way of easing us into an acceptance of that loss. But prolonged denial can lead us to self-destruction, as we saw in Clara's story. I daresay that at the root of almost every addict's or alcoholic's tragic struggle is the denial of pain. Addiction and alcoholism are just two of the many consequences of what happens when our pain and suffering are not healed through the Forgiveness Cycle.

Whether we are grieving the loss of a loved one, a marriage, a job, a treasured hope, or some other measure of our self-worth, when we allow ourselves to feel the pain, we can quickly move to anger. We feel anger at others, at ourselves, or at God for letting such cruelty occur in our world. In that hospital room, the young mother expressed her anger. But having spoken her rage, she was able to move through and beyond her anger. Anger may have its say in the present, but it does not have the ability to change the past, and it rarely satisfies our true desires in the future. If I feel anger, I am human; if I stay locked in my anger, I am a prisoner.

The next stage in the grief process, bargaining, is another form of nonacceptance, much like denial. If only I did this, said that, went one way instead of another, this loss would not have happened, this pain would not have been felt. "If I were a better mother, if I had stayed home instead of going to my meeting," the woman in the hospital had bargained, "then my child would have been safe." We can't bargain away our hurt, our guilt, our shame, or the reality of our loss. The only way out of what hurts is through it. Bargaining is not the same as learning from our experiences and letting them transform us. Healing is unconditional. Unfortunately, we don't get to dictate the terms of our healing.

Depression in the grief process is an understandable reaction to the realization that life has changed, often in painful or even tragic ways. How do we go on when a loved one has died? How do we find joy when a spouse has left us? Where is the hope when a prognosis is terminal? So how do we move beyond this shattering grief? We find our hope and our healing in the final stage of the grieving process: acceptance.

Acceptance is the recognition that things have changed and will never be what they were before. This is how we can find the strength to journey on. We accept the truth of what happened. We accept our hurt, our anguish, our sadness, our anger, our shame, and in doing so we accept our own vulnerability. This recognition of our vulnerability is vital. As we saw in chapter 3, "Understanding the Fourfold Path," there are only two choices when we are faced with a loss. We can put our hands on our hearts and accept our suffering, our vulnerability, and our human frailty. Or we can reject this suffering, this vulnerability, this frailty, and raise our fists for revenge. As we will see in the next chapter, it is our shared humanity, our shared losses, and our shared grief that ultimately allow us to reconnect again with the world around us. We are harmed together, and we heal together. It is only in this fragile web of relationship that we rediscover our purpose, meaning, and joy after pain and loss. The web will break time and time again, but we can rebuild it. Only in restoring the web of connection can we find peace. I'm sure it is possible to heal in a mountaintop cave alone, but for most of us the quickest and deepest healing happens in the embrace of others.

When we deny our feelings, when we choose not to name our hurts and instead reject the pain of our losses, we always end up seeking destruction. It may be self-destruction, as Clara experienced in her efforts to numb her unacknowledged pain. We may enter the cycle of revenge in a forlorn hope that hurting others will fix our pain. It does not. The only way to stop the pain is to accept it. The only way to accept it is to name it and, by naming it, to feel it fully. In so doing, you discover that your pain is part of the great, eternal tapestry of human loss and heartbreak. You realize you are not alone in your suffering, that others have experienced and survived what you have experienced, and that you too can survive and know joy and happiness again. When you embrace your feelings, you embrace yourself and allow others to embrace you too.

No Feeling Is Wrong

As victims share the many shades of their feelings and losses, there can be no debate. As Father Lapsley says in his wonderful book, *Redeeming the Past,* "People must be encouraged to feel to the fullest, no matter how uncomfortable. . . . People need space to be weak and vulnerable for a time before they can become strong."[9] This is true no matter what has hurt you, no matter what you have lost, no matter what anyone says you "should" be feeling and for how long.

When Mpho came to me with the anguish of Angela's murder, I had to create a space for her pain and her grief. There was so much loss, and I so badly wished to make it go away or fix it somehow. I had to accept that this was not possible, that I could not undo the brutality of Angela's murder, or the sorrow and loss that seemed too overwhelming for our family to endure. All I could do was listen as Mpho named the many ways she and so many others were hurting:

I had no idea of all the pieces involved in living through something like this. It takes a demolition to see the bones of a building. It's like somebody had blasted away the veneer and I could see all the tracery of connections. We are so deeply connected to one another—our family, Angela, Angela's family. The reverberations are vast and ceaseless.

I had landed in grief and guilt. I heard the screams of Angela's mother and children on the phone. How do you ever recover from hearing that kind of anguish, those wails of pain and loss? But I felt it was my responsibility to tell them. I knew the news of her death had to come from me. I honestly don't know how to stand in my pain and in the pain of Angela's family. I feel like, to them, I will forever be associated with death because I was the one to deliver the news. They had so many questions, and it was so difficult because they didn't get to see her. I saw her. Angela had traveled so far away from her children and family to make a better life for them all, and this had happened. She worked for me and there is this great sense of guilt. If I hadn't hired her, would she still be alive?

At first there was just grief and guilt, but then the fury came. This person not only stole Angela's life, he stole our freedom and our sense of safety, our sense of place, and even our home. We can never go back there. The items he stole from the house are nothing compared to stealing all our happy memories. Our home isn't a home anymore; it's a crime scene. Nyaniso can't think of her bedroom without thinking of violence and murder. How do you ever recover that sense of safety? It's just gone.

The fury still comes and goes. I hear so many voices and questions in my head. Onalenna asking where Auntie Angela is and if she's okay. Asking me if the bad person is going to come back, and I know what she is really asking is if she is

*safe, if she is going to be hurt. I hear Nyaniso crying and
saying she just wants to wake up, begging me to wake her
up from this nightmare. And I can't wake her up because the
nightmare is real. I feel like I've lost the power to protect my
children and keep them safe. I was so afraid this had broken
Nyaniso. How did evil get so close to my children? How did
I let it get so near? As a mother, it's a horrible feeling. I can't
make the world safe for them. It makes everything feel so
out of control. I have so much fear and so much anxiety and
always this sadness and grief mixed in and touching everything and everyone.*

My heart ached beyond measure to see my daughter and
my grandchildren in such pain. Listening to Mpho's suffering, I had to stop my impulse to try to make it better, to
fix it, and to try to take her suffering away. The only way
I could really help was just to listen and offer my presence
and my love. Mpho was understandably worried about the
impact on Nyaniso of having Angela murdered in her room.
This would be a horror for anyone. A friend recommended
that Mpho and Nyaniso speak with a trauma therapist. The
therapist told Nyaniso that it made perfect sense that she
would want to deal with her painful feelings by pretending it was a dream and that this was a valid choice. She also
explained that choosing reality was another choice, and asked
Nyaniso which choice would ultimately serve her better and
be the most helpful and best place from which to heal.

By validating Nyaniso's feelings without any judgment or
logical argument to the contrary, Nyaniso felt acknowledged
and safe to move forward through her grief and pain, and she

How to Acknowledge the Harm

- Listen.
- Do not try to fix the pain.
- Do not minimize the loss.
- Do not offer advice.
- Do not respond with your own loss or grief.
- Keep confidentiality.
- Offer your love and your caring.
- Empathize and offer comfort.

chose the path that would best serve her healing. It is not easy or comfortable to listen to the painful feelings of our loved ones or the people we care about, but if we are to help them, we must do so without reservation and from a place of love and caring.

When we are hurting, we all must do as Nyaniso did and make a choice to move forward from denial of the pain to acceptance of the harm. We cannot truly bear the pain alone. We heal together, and when we share the burden of our brokenness, quite amazingly we find we are less broken. Our hearts get lighter and our wounds begin to heal. Find someone who will listen and acknowledge the harm you feel, and pour out your sorrow until you are utterly empty.

With Whom Do We Share?

Do we need to tell every single person every single hurt feeling we feel? Of course not. Only you will know the hurts that linger and fester. Only you can take the measure of your own suffering, and only you will know with whom to invest your confidence. I encourage you to voice the hurt you feel as soon as possible. The hurt will always find expression. Whether it is directed inward and causes you suffering or is directed outward and hurts those close to you, the hurt will not lie down. You may not have had a choice in being harmed, but you can always choose to be healed.

As we mentioned in the previous chapter, in an ideal world the ones who hurt us would come to us, admit their wrong, and witness the anguish they have caused. We, in turn, would share the depth of our loss and pain and grief with them. We would ask our questions, receive satisfactory and complete answers, understand, forgive, and renew the relationships. Apologies would be offered, remorse expressed, justice served, and reparations made. But the path of forgiveness rarely follows this ideal model.

And what do we do if the person who hurt us has passed away? This is the case with my father. There are some questions I wish I could ask him, but I will never be able to. And what if we don't know who hurt us? Like Mpho and her family, so many people live with unresolved cases of murder, are victims of terrorist attacks, or have been violated by unknown assailants. What if to see the person who caused us harm would end up hurting us more? What if that person does not care that they have hurt us? What if that person does not yet know how desperately they need our forgiveness? What if the person who hurt us will not or cannot listen? Can we still name the hurt? The answer is yes.

In many cases, the cause of our suffering is a group, a

government, or an institution. Today, the refugees in South Sudan live in terror of the Janjaweed militia; in Syria, the bombing and terror has become a daily event; Afghanistan has endured decades of war, occupation, and oppression; in South Africa, though apartheid has disappeared from our statute books, its effects continue to impede our progress. The South Sudan militia, the Syrian government, the warring factions and invading forces in Afghanistan, and the former South African regime are all institutions, not individuals. Is it still possible to walk the path of forgiving? The answer is again, yes.

If you cannot, or choose not to, name your hurt to the perpetrator, then you can talk to a trusted friend or family member, a spiritual advisor, a counselor, another who has experienced the same kind of harm, or anyone who will not judge you and who will be able to listen with love and empathy. Just as in telling the story, you can write your hurt down in a letter or journal. The most important thing is to share with someone who is able to receive your feelings without judging or shaming you for having them. Indeed, because it is never easy to confront the one who has harmed us directly, I strongly encourage you to name the hurt to others first.

Finding Your Voice

When we give voice to our hurt, it loses its stranglehold on our lives and our identities. It stops being the central character in our stories. Ultimately, as we will discuss in the next chapter, the act of forgiving helps us create a new story. Forgiveness lets us become the author of our own future, unfettered by the past. But in order to begin to tell a new story, we must first have the courage to speak. Mpho is brave to speak of her hurt. It is human to want to retaliate, to feel anger, and to feel a profound sense of resentment toward those who have harmed us. When we share these feelings, however, when we give voice to our desire for revenge, our rage, and the many ways we feel our dignity has been violated, the desire for revenge lessens. There is relief. Feeling this relief does not mean that there is no justice, or that it was okay for someone to hurt us. It simply means we don't have to let our suffering make us perpetual victims. When we name the hurt, just as when we tell the story, we are in the process of reclaiming our dignity and building something new from the wreckage of what was lost.

Learning to Feel and Learning to Forgive

Many people are disconnected from their feelings and their own experiences. This is often the result of old suffering that has caused us to numb ourselves. For this reason we must sometimes relearn to feel. Reclaiming our ability to feel is essential for learning to forgive. I have found it often helps to take a few quiet moments at the end of a day or the end of a week and take an inventory, to see if I am holding on to any fresh resentment or harboring any new hurts. When I take a few quiet moments to reflect, it is easier to feel if I am in pain. Often I am not even conscious of the hurt, but I may find it has lodged itself in my body. Sometimes an unspoken hurt feels like anxiety or an uneasiness in my stomach—this can be a sign of fear. Sometimes the silenced pain is experienced as tightness in my chest or a feeling that tears are sitting close behind my eyes—this can be sadness or shame. If the body feels unusually tired or heavy, this can be depression. Any of these can be indicators that there is some work to be done and some hurts still to be named.

We choose to heal and we choose to move forward by being brave and vulnerable enough to feel. While human emotions are universal, they often exist below our consciousness. The emotional regions of the brain, scientists remind us, are older than the intellectual regions of the brain. We had feelings before we could express them. This is often still the case. We don't always have the vocabulary to express our feelings. The more conversant and comfortable you can be with your emotions, the richer your experience of life will be, and the more capable you will be of forgiving.

We Are All Family

In the midst of her pain and grief, Mpho was able to feel a profound connection and solidarity with others whose homes and sense of safety had been violated, with other victims of violent crime, and with all the parents in the world worrying about their children's physical and emotional safety and well-being. This connection in shared suffering is a great source of comfort when we are in pain.

It may be easier to name the hurt when it comes to those family and friends closest to us. The hurt often cuts deeper when someone we love causes it, but the risk that comes with naming the hurt may not be as great. We all have blind spots. We all have moments when we behave without thought for other people's feelings. Even if we thought carefully about every action, we could never anticipate how all people will react. Mpho and her best friend often unwittingly hurt each other, but Mpho explains, "It is an incredible gift to have a friend who will lovingly hold up a mirror to my blind spots. Lovingly does not necessarily mean gently or painlessly. My best friend and I have had some of the worst, most searingly painful fights. But we have learned to name our hurts and name them quickly. Often we find that the one doesn't know the other is hurt or even recognize that a comment or action could be construed as hurtful. Naming our hurts is how we keep the fabric of our friendship whole." It is inevitable that we will hurt one another; so the sooner we mend the frayed fabric of our love the better.

By being vulnerable and courageous enough to name their hurts, Mpho and her friend have found a way to keep their relationship healthy and avoid having old grudges fester. We must learn to do this with both those who are closest to us and those we encounter in our neighborhoods and communities. Our lives are entwined with one another, friend and supposed enemy, loved one and stranger, each and every day. We are one human family. As members of one family, we will inevitably hurt each other—sometimes horribly, sometimes unimaginably, and sometimes irrevocably. Yet as members of one family, for us to flourish there must be forgiveness. There must be healing.

As we will see in the next chapter, we can discover our shared humanity and write a new story of transformation, even in the midst of the most profound suffering. We have told the story and named the hurt. Forgiveness will transform both our story and our suffering.

Let us pause now and listen to what the heart hears.

Meet me here
Speak my name
I am not your enemy
I am your teacher
I may even be your friend
Let us tell our truth together, you and I
My name is anger: I say you have been wronged
My name is shame: my story is your hidden pain
My name is fear: my story is vulnerability
My name is resentment: I say things should have been different
My name is grief
My name is depression
My name is heartache
My name is anxiety
I have many names
And many lessons
I am not your enemy
I am your teacher

Summary
Naming the Hurt

- Identify the feelings within the facts.
- Remember, no feeling is wrong, bad, or invalid.
- Recognize the stages of grief, and honor wherever you fall in the process.
- Find someone who will acknowledge you and listen to your feelings without trying to fix them.
- Accept your own vulnerability.
- Move forward when you are ready.

Meditation

Validation

1. Return to your safe space. Note again what it looks, sounds, and feels like. If need be, wrap your cloak of safety around you.
2. Now welcome back your trusted and affirming companion.
3. Put one hand on your heart and the other on your belly. Take a deep breath and relax. When you return to the hurt, notice what feelings arise. Share these emotions with your companion. Stay with the emotion. Experience and express how you feel about what happened.
4. Each emotion is appropriate and valid.
5. Hear your companion affirm the truth and pain of your feelings.
6. When you have heard and accepted this validation, settle back into your place of safety and rest.
7. When you are ready, you may leave your safe space.

Stone Ritual

Clenching the Stone

1. Take your stone in your dominant hand.
2. Name out loud a hurt you are feeling. As you name it, clench the stone in your hand.
3. Open your hand. As you release your fist, release the hurt.
4. Clench and release the stone again as you name each of your hurts.

Journal Exercise

The Grief Journal

1. Write down all the things you have lost. What did you lose? Did you lose your trust? Did you lose your safety? Did you lose your dignity? Did you lose someone whom you loved? Did you lose something that you cherished?
2. Now name the feelings that accompany these losses. *I am angry. I am sad. I am heartbroken. I am afraid.* Feel free to use your own words. What does your heart tell you? What is the weight of this loss? Name it so you can heal it.

Chapter 6

Granting Forgiveness

WE HAVE SO MANY BIG STORIES of forgiveness. This book is full of stories of people who have had the courage to forgive after a devastating loss or a heinous crime. We admire these people. We wish we could be more like them. The truth is that the people who are able to offer these overwhelming gifts of forgiveness are people like you and me. Some of them have discovered a well of compassion at a moment of need. But many of them are people who have exercised that forgiveness muscle in the small daily acts of forgiveness that make family life more than merely tolerable and give us access to joy as we walk in the world. The repeated exercise of forgiveness, offered in small ways, means that a pattern is already in place when, or if, one must confront an unspeakable need.

Raising children has sometimes felt like training for a forgiveness marathon. Like other parents, Leah and I could create a whole catalogue of the failures and irritations our children have served up. As infants, their loud squalls disturbed our slumber. Even as one or the other of us stumbled out of bed, the irritation at being woken and the thoughts of the fatigue that would lie like a pall over the coming day gave way to the simple acknowledgment that this was a baby. This is what babies do. The loving parent slides easily into the place of acceptance, even gratitude, for the helpless bundle of tears. Toddler tantrums might provoke an answering anger in a mother or father, but anger will be quickly replaced by the understanding that a little person does not yet have the language to express the flood of feelings contained in his or her body. Acceptance comes.

As our own children grew, they found new (and remarkably creative) ways of testing our patience, our resolve, and our rules and limits. We learned time and again to use the teaching moments their transgressions offered. But mostly we learned to forgive them over and over again, and fold them back into our embrace. We know our children are so much more than the sum of everything they have done wrong. Their stories are more than rehearsals of their repeated need for forgiveness. We know that even the things they did wrong were opportunities for us to teach them to be citizens of the world. We have been able to forgive them because we have known their humanity. We have seen the good in them. We have prayed for them. It was easy to pray for them. They are our children. It is easy to want the best for them.

But I also pray for other people who may irk or hurt me. When my heart holds anger or resentment toward someone, I pray for that person's well-being. It is a powerful practice and has often opened the doorway to finding forgiveness. People have sometimes expressed shock that I prayed daily for the president of South Africa, even during the darkest days of apartheid, but how could I not? I was praying for him to rediscover his humanity, and thereby for our country to rediscover its shared humanity.

His Holiness the Dalai Lama has a meditation he calls "Giving and Taking." He visualizes sending his enemies his positive emotions, such as happiness, affection, and love, and he visualizes receiving their negative emotions—what he calls their poisons: hatred, fear, and cruelty. He takes care not to blame or judge their actions. He breathes in their poisons and breathes out his compassion and forgiveness. This is how he reduces hatred and how he cultivates a forgiving mind. All our grievances are part of a larger story, and when we can understand this greater drama and the humanity of all involved, our anguish and anger are diminished.

Choosing to Forgive

After we tell our stories and name our hurts, the next step is to grant forgiveness. Sometimes this choice happens quickly and sometimes it happens slowly, but inevitably it is how we move forward along the Fourfold Path. We choose forgiveness because it is how we find freedom and keep from remaining trapped in an endless loop of telling our stories and naming our hurts. It is how we move from victim to hero. A victim is in a position of weakness and subject to the whims of others. Heroes are people who determine their own fate and their own future. A victim has nothing to give and no choices to make. A hero has the strength and ability to be generous and forgiving, and the power and freedom that come from being able to make the choice to grant forgiveness.

In some cases, we find forgiveness after a long time, and sometimes forgiveness finds us even in the midst of our grief. For Kia Scherr, learning of the terrorist attacks in Mumbai, where her husband and thirteen-year-old daughter were visiting, forgiveness was the last thing on her mind:

> What do you do when the worst thing that could possibly happen actually happens? In November of 2008 my husband, Alan, and daughter, Naomi, traveled to Mumbai for a meditation retreat at the Oberoi Hotel.
>
> On November 14 I said good-bye to Alan and Naomi at the Dulles airport in Virginia. We kept in touch through e-mail and phone calls over the next week, and on November 24 I had my last conversation with them. Naomi had just gotten her nose pierced and had sent photos through the e-mail. She was so excited as I shared the news that her test scores had come in for her entrance examination to a top girls boarding school in New York. She had scored 95 percent overall and was full of joy when I told her the news. Alan and I excitedly discussed all of this, and our last words to each other were "I love you."
>
> The next day I got on a plane to Tampa, Florida, to visit my parents, sons, brothers, and sister for our Thanksgiving holiday. When I checked my e-mail the following day, there were no messages from Alan or Naomi. Later that afternoon the phone rang. It was the managing director of Synchronicity Foundation, which was sponsoring the meditation retreat in Mumbai. She told me to turn on

the news right away because the Oberoi Hotel was being attacked by terrorists. I dropped the phone in disbelief. For the next two days I watched in horror as the terror attack in Mumbai went on and on and on. I had no idea where Alan and Naomi were and prayed that they were safe in their rooms. Friends and family called, joined our prayers, and called upon their friends to pray with us.

Because Alan and Naomi were unaccounted for, my eldest son, Aaron, sent their photos to CNN, in case they were unconscious somewhere in Mumbai with no identification on them. E-mails began pouring in from all over the world. We felt comforted by this loving support from so-called strangers. At six A.M. on Friday, November 28, I received a call from the U.S. Consulate in Mumbai confirming that my husband and daughter had both been shot and killed in the Tiffen restaurant at the Oberoi Hotel.

For the next few hours my family and I sat together on the living room sofa, numb and in shock. As we watched the aftermath on CNN we saw that there was one lone surviving terrorist. As I looked at his photo on the television screen, the words of Jesus Christ came to me: "Father, forgive them, they know not what they do." I wasn't a religious person, but these were the words I heard. In that moment, I turned to my family and said, "We must forgive them." Everyone was shocked. They thought I had lost my mind. But at that moment I just said what I felt to be true. I felt a ray of peace enter my heart, and I knew it was the right thing to do. I knew the only way I could go on living was to forgive the terrorists. In those moments, I knew that forgiveness was essential, so I forgave. "There is already enough hate," I told my family. "We must send our love and compassion." I knew that to respond with love to an act of terror was the only way to triumph over terrorism.

I have learned that my forgiveness required a deep level of acceptance of what had occurred. This does not mean agreement with or any kind of pardoning or condoning of the action that hurt me. It simply means acceptance of the reality of the situation and letting go of the incident, which cannot be changed. Once I accepted that my husband and daughter had been killed by terrorists, I could move forward to heal. This acceptance brought me to an inner peace that cannot be shattered. Within this peace is the essence of a humanity we all share. It is a choice I make every day.

This does not mean that justice must not be served. Actions have consequences and those who commit such acts of violence must be held accountable to the full extent of the law. The terrorist was executed, as per the laws of Mumbai. It cuts me to the depths of my being when I think of the disconnect that had to have happened within these young men to be capable of such destruction. What confusion and deluded thinking led to this misguided behavior? I think about his mother and how she too must have suffered when her son was killed. In this way, we are the same. We are connected.

Forgiveness has allowed me to keep my heart open and soft. I chose to forgive because I knew that if I did not, the unforgiving would have kept me closed and hardened inside. I made an instantaneous choice when Alan and Naomi were murdered to let go of anger, hatred, and any desire for retaliation.

This is true transformation. When we unleash the power of unconditional love, we create an environment for positive change. There is still a world of possibility, even when the worst thing happens that could possibly happen. Forgiveness gives me the capacity to contribute something of value—to create a positive outcome to a terrible tragedy. I have lost Alan and Naomi, but I now know I will spend the rest of my life inviting people around the world to open to the experience of peace, love, and compassion through the power of forgiveness. Our survival as a human race depends on it. It was not my choice to have this horrific experience. But it is my choice as to what happens next.[10]

Recognizing Shared Humanity

We are able to forgive because we are able to recognize our shared humanity. We are able to recognize that we are all fragile, vulnerable, flawed human beings capable of thoughtlessness and cruelty. We also recognize that no one is born evil and that we are all more than the worst thing we have done in our lives. A human life is a great mixture of goodness, beauty, cruelty, heartbreak, indifference, love, and so much more. We want to divide the good from the bad, the saints from the sinners, but we cannot. All of us share the core qualities of our human nature, and so sometimes we are generous and sometimes selfish. Sometimes we are thoughtful and other times thoughtless, sometimes we are kind and sometimes cruel. This is not a belief. This is a fact.

If we look at any hurt, we can see a larger context in which the hurt happened. If we look at any perpetrator, we can discover a story that tells us something about what led up to that person causing harm. It doesn't justify the person's actions; it does provide some context. We discover our shared humanity by seeing our connection rather than our separation. Kia Scherr was able to recognize her connection to the terrorist's mother, and her suffering, and show extraordinary compassion even for the misguided men who killed her husband and daughter.

It is worth repeating, since it is so easy to forget: No one is born a liar or a rapist or a terrorist. No one is born full of hatred. No one is born full of violence. No one is born in any less glory or goodness than you or I. But on any given day, in any given situation, in any painful life experience, this glory and goodness can be forgotten, obscured, or lost. We can easily be hurt and broken, and it is good to remember that we can just as easily be the ones who have done the hurting and the breaking.

We are all members of the same human family. This is not just a metaphor; this is a literal statement of fact. All modern humans are related to what scientists call Mitochondrial Eve; this refers to our common matrilineal ancestor. She lived approximately two hundred thousand years ago, and depending on how you estimate the length of a generation, we are only five to ten thousand generations from one another. To put it another way, each of us is a cousin of one another at most ten thousand times removed. And yes, Mitochondrial Eve lived in Africa, so in a very real way we are all Africans, which—given the racist propaganda that has been put forward for so long in many parts of our world—is a bit ironic, don't you think?[11]

When I am particularly affronted, injured, or angered, it helps to remember our shared humanity. For Kia, it helped to know that the terrorist who shot her husband and daughter also had a mother who grieved his death. It also helps to remember that we are all part of a context that so often determines, or at least greatly influences, our actions and choices. This does not excuse them; it simply helps to explain them. For me, it helped to know that, in the Karoo when we had stopped for ice cream, the boy at the market was simply reciting the script of hatred and intolerance he had been taught to memorize. For Lynn and Dan Wagner, who lost their daughters in a car accident, it helped to know that the woman behind the wheel of the other car was a mother who loved her own two children. In seeing the many ways we are similar and how our lives are inextricably linked, we can find empathy and compassion. In finding empathy and compassion, we are able to move in the direction of forgiving.

We are, every one of us, so very flawed and so very fragile. I know that, were I born a member of the white ruling class at that time in South Africa's past, I might easily have treated someone with the same dismissive disdain with which I was treated. I know, given the same pressures and circumstances, I am capable of the same monstrous acts as any other human on this achingly beautiful planet. It is this knowledge of my own frailty that helps me find my compassion, my empathy, my similarity, and my forgiveness for the frailty and cruelty of others. We have seen that in order to forgive it is important we accept the facts of what happened and the feelings we felt about what happened. We have accepted our own human vulnerability and frailty. Now we must accept the vulnerability and frailty of the one who harmed us.

True Forgiveness

Such simple words—*I forgive you*—but often they are so hard to say and even harder to mean. Perhaps you believe you have already accepted what has happened and forgiven the person who harmed you. This is wonderful. In fairness, I must caution that many people, even very spiritual people, try to leap over their suffering in pursuit of their inner peace or their sense of what is the right thing to do. The words of forgiveness are said, but the reality of forgiveness has not taken root in their hearts and lives. "Darling, I am so sorry. Do you forgive me?" says the contrite wife, walking in late from work and finding dinner dried out on the table. "Yes," her husband spits back through gritted teeth, seeing his hours of loving preparation wasted. Without allowing themselves to walk the Forgiveness Cycle, the couple establishes a veneer of peace that is more of an uneasy truce than a genuine forgiveness. This is a small example, but it can be even more the case when facing the greater wounds we may suffer. Look deeply into your heart and make sure that when you say "I forgive you," you have truly confronted your own past. If you do, your future will truly be free.

How do we know when we grant forgiveness that we truly mean it? How do we know when true forgiveness has taken root in our hearts and minds? I wish I could give you a one-size-fits-all answer. For some it feels as if a huge weight has been lifted. For others it is an overwhelming feeling of peace. Often it can simply be that you know you have forgiven when you wish the other person well, and if you can't wish them well, you at least no longer wish them harm. As we have said, there is freedom in forgiveness, and when you feel this new freedom, you know you have truly forgiven.

For Ben Bosinger, it felt like he had heard a million times over that he should forgive his father. He heard it from friends and therapists, from family members and priests. He listened to a million "shoulds" about forgiving, but he didn't know what it really meant to forgive. He didn't know how you actually forgave someone, what it looked like or felt like. He tried saying it out loud, but it didn't feel real on the inside. He believed for over thirty years that he would never truly be able to forgive:

> For the first eleven years of my life all I remember is fear. Not like a fear of falling and getting hurt or the fear you feel when you know you are in trouble for something. It was life-or-death fear. Sheer terror every moment. I feared for my life, and for the lives of my brothers and sister, and for the life of my mother. My father was the angriest, most violent human I have ever known. He didn't simply hit me. He beat me. He humiliated me. He tortured me. And he did the same to my seven siblings, locking one brother in the car for days as a punishment. I remember this one time my little brother was only about four or five. He was playing with his blocks and my father picked him up by the hair, by his scalp. Something about the blocks angered my dad so badly that he held my baby brother up by his scalp and shook him. I remember his screams. I was so terrified for my brother, watching him dangling in midair in so much pain, thinking that the top of his head was going to rip clean away. I also remember the shame of being relieved

that it wasn't me. I hated my dad in that moment so much I could have killed him. I hated him for hating us so much.

There was no place to hide and no place to run. There was no safety. When the police came because school called or a neighbor called, they never did anything. No one could stop him, and it felt like no one even cared enough to try. I don't know why it took my mom twenty-five years to finally take us and leave him. I don't know why no one protected me. Not the police, not teachers, not neighbors. I vowed that someday I would make him pay. I grew up angry and violent myself. My brothers were angry and violent as well. How could we not be? It was what we were raised on, what we were fed and nurtured with. When you have a grown man punching you in the face as hard as he can every day just because he can, a man who is supposed to love and protect you, how do you ever forgive? I didn't know why I was even born. As I got older, I decided that life was about beating others down before they beat me down. I had turned into my own father, and I couldn't forgive him for that either.

This anger I carried around, this lack of trust in people, affected every relationship I ever had. Eventually I turned this anger into self-destruction. I didn't have my father beating on me every day, but I beat on myself. I knew I was worthless, and I turned to drugs and alcohol, I picked fights, I lashed out at anyone who even dared to show me love or affection. After ten years, I stopped drinking and drugging, but I was still angry and bitter and lashing out at the people I cared about. So many people told me to forgive my father, but I couldn't see how this could possibly make me happy. I felt that if I forgave him I would be just one more person letting him off the hook for his behavior. The only way I had to pay him back for what he did to me was to withhold my love from him. Once I had my daughter and became a father myself, I was even angrier at him for not being the father I needed, and I was angry at him because I blamed him for my own shortcomings as a husband and a father. How could I possibly forgive him? He had destroyed my childhood and now he was responsible for destroying my daughter's childhood. Every problem I had in life was because of him. I resented him and I resented myself. And still everyone around me, people I had learned to trust and rely on for guidance, told me that the only way out of my misery was by forgiving my dad.

He has never said he was sorry for what he did to me, to our family. He has never explained why he was so violent or angry. I have no idea how he could beat and torture his own flesh and blood and seem to find so much joy in the process. I used to think he wasn't human. I used to pretend he didn't exist. Eventually I realized that I was carrying him with me everywhere I went, into every intimate relationship, and even into my own parenting. It was this more than anything, I think, that made me simply turn my motorcycle up his driveway one afternoon. I was sick and tired of being sick and tired. The pain of constantly carrying him with me was finally greater than the pain of the beatings I took as a child. Something had to give.

It was something bigger than me that made me forgive him. One day I drove up his driveway and he came outside and we talked about motorcycles. We both really like motorcycles. And in that instant, when we both were bent down looking at that greasy engine, side by side, I forgave him. I looked at his long gray hair, his wrinkled face, his obvious weakening from hard living and old age. He was human. He was so flawed. He loved motorcycles just like me, and somewhere in the middle of seeing all that, I simply forgave him. It was like this huge boulder was lifted off my chest and I could finally breathe again. He didn't ask me to forgive him. He wasn't sorry or remorseful. Still, I forgave.

We didn't skip off into the sunset together. In fact, years later I saw him again and he said something to me that felt hurtful and critical, and for a moment I wondered if the forgiveness had worn off. Instead, I learned that I had an expectation that my forgiveness would magically turn him into a nice guy, a different guy, a better guy. And with this expectation I was making myself a victim to him all over again. The magic didn't happen to him. The magic happened to me. I felt lighter. The world seemed a more hopeful place. I learned not to take things so personally, and I learned that I was the only one responsible for what kind of father I turned out to be to my children. I wasted decades of my life reliving the victimization I endured as a child. When I forgave my father, it all melted away. I was free. Forgiveness didn't save him or let him off the hook. It saved me.

Telling a New Story

Ben's story is about how he went from a victim to a hero. No longer embittered, he is now ennobled by his own experience of forgiving his abuser. More important, he is finally free of the abuse and free to create a new story of fatherhood within his own family. Ben is no longer bound to the extreme violence he suffered as a child, and in breaking those chains, he now tells a new story of what it means to be a father. It is a story in which he is no longer a victim, although his father certainly victimized him and his siblings. It is a story in which he is now a hero and can be a hero for his daughter.

In writing this book, we consulted with many of the leading experts on forgiveness around the world, men and women who have devoted their lives to helping people heal and to studying the forgiveness process. Every one of them said how important it is to be able to tell a new story and how this ability is a sign of healing and wholeness.

What exactly does it mean to tell a new story? There are, no doubt, countless ways in which your story changes. We have seen this in Ben's story and in so many of the others. Your story is no longer just about the facts of what happened, or about the pain and hurt you suffered. It is a story that recognizes the story of the one who hurt you, however misguided that person was. It is a story that recognizes our shared humanity. Ben was able to see his father's humanity, even in a small thing like a shared interest in motorcycles. He was able to see his father's humanity in his gray hair and his wrinkled face. This shared humanity allowed him to tell a new story.

In Ben's new story, he was not the victim of the story but the victor. It is important to be clear: Ben was victimized, and in many ways he was a victim of his father's violence. By saying he was a hero does not take this pain or suffering away or, God forbid, blame him for it in some way. People are victims of all kinds of atrocities. We are not trying to deny this reality. What is incredible when we listen to so many of these people recount their stories is how they are able to retell them in a way that is filled with courage and compassion. They are able to explain what happened to them in a way that reveals how it has ennobled rather than embittered them.

The guarantee in life is that we will suffer. What is not guaranteed is how we will respond, whether we will let this suffering embitter us or ennoble us. This is our choice. How do we allow our suffering to ennoble us? We make meaning out of it and make it matter. We use our experiences as many of the people in this book have used theirs: to make ourselves into richer, deeper, more empathic people. We may, like the people you meet in this book, work to prevent such harm from happening to others. Only you can decide how to tell a new story. You are the author of your life, and only you can write *your* book of forgiving.

Our Story

Mpho's story began with a horrific act that left my immediate family shaken to the core. Mpho continues to walk the Fourfold Path of forgiveness and reveals her own challenges in forgiving the man who stands accused of Angela's murder:

> *It isn't as if the feelings go away once they are named. This is so important to realize. The Fourfold Path isn't a path where you step off one piece and step completely onto another. I guess you could say I stayed halfway between naming the hurt and forgiving. It was a real relief to say I'm angry about the loss of life, the unnecessary cruelty, the violation, and I feel guilty because I think maybe if I had gone back to the house two hours earlier, or maybe if I had picked up some clue that things were amiss, I could have prevented this from*

happening. I feel guilty that Angela was murdered while she was living in my house and taking care of my children, and what about her house and her children? Mostly, I'm so very sad this person is gone from our lives and her family's lives. I'm really sad Angela died in such a brutal and cruel way. I'm sad I couldn't give her a proper good-bye, and I'm sad that this happened in my home.

But somewhere within discovering the texture and quality of my hurts, of pulling apart the strands of what I was feeling and giving them the attention they needed, I also realized that I'm sad for the person who killed her. Right from the beginning, for whatever reason, I imagined the murderer to be a man, and thought he is going to have to live with this death for the rest of his life. Can you imagine what it would take for someone to kill another person so brutally and not have it affect his psyche? When you harm another, you also harm yourself. His humanity suffered from his own inhumane act.

I can tell you this feeling of sadness and empathy for the murderer was something of a shock to me, and I believe this was my personal open door to forgiving. I didn't know his entire story, but I knew there must be a story there. However, it was only after I engaged in all the formal rituals for grieving and leaned on those who could validate my anger and fear, and after I was able to connect with my community and all who came together to share my loss with me, that I was able to consider his story and consider forgiveness. There is incredible power in ritual, and you see this as people come with flowers and candles when there is mass death and tragic loss. This is what we do, and it is so healing. We need rituals for all traumas and loss, whether it is betrayal or infidelity or violence or murder. *Ritual helps us heal, and ritual helped me heal and become ready to consider the person who murdered Angela, his story, his pain. Ultimately, I knew I had to find a way to rewrite the story of our connection so that my family did not remain trussed and bound to the carnage this person created.*

The man who, now as I write this, stands accused of Angela's murder is someone I knew and someone connected to our family and to Angela in so many ways. He was our gardener. He was only twenty-two when he allegedly committed this murder. Can you even imagine what makes a young man act in such a brutal way? He shares, oddly enough, the same birthday as Angela. Their birthday was on a Sunday, and on Monday he had come to our home in the morning to share our birthday ritual of having cake for breakfast. This was in December, just months before it is alleged that he came back to the house to commit this crime. His mom used to work for my mom, and it was this connection that made me employ him to work in our garden. Initially we had quite a bit of work in the garden for him to do, so he worked for us three days a week, but then it got to the point where I didn't need him that much—only one day a week was all that was really needed—but I wanted to keep him working, to help him out, so I paid for the extra two days. He also did some handyman things around the house.

A couple of weeks before Angela was killed he disappeared, stopped showing up for work. Before that he had been hanging a curtain rod in my room and had asked Angela what it was that was wrapped up in a cupboard in my room. She had told him it was a computer, and from the way it was wrapped there was no way to tell what it was or that it was valuable. This computer ended up being the only thing missing from the house when Angela was killed. It makes you think about the chain of events. What if I had never had him hang a curtain rod? What if the cupboard door had been closed? Would Angela still be alive?

His sister was also great friends with Nyaniso. I have this photo of them together that has been on my refrigerator for years. His family was connected to mine. Through my mother. Through my daughter. This is why I hired him. But increasingly he had a hard time showing up for work. Our families are connected now in a new way, and I feel for them, for his mother's grief and loss. No one wants this. There can be no sides when you are standing in the middle of wreckage.

I should say that he hasn't confessed. He hasn't admitted to this crime. He hasn't been convicted. No one knows yet who murdered Angela, but whoever it is stole our home and constructed this new place of fear we've had to live in. If it is indeed the gardener, I know something of his story. Because we have these places where our lives cross, I can recognize our shared humanity. I can feel sorrow for the choices he made in his life. I can find my way to understanding. I feel for his family. Even when no one had been charged for Angela's murder, I felt sorrow for whoever had done this horrible thing. I feel sorrow for anyone who commits such a brutal act of violence, and sorrow for our world in general. And if I'm truly honest, I know there is not as much separating us as I'd like to imagine.

Most of the time I feel as if I've forgiven the killer. I don't wish this person his comeuppance. I feel profoundly sad for this person and for all of us. I've accepted the facts of what happened and the ripple effects of the trauma. There are moments, however, when the trauma of Angela's death resurfaces in our family, and I feel all the anger and rage and sadness acutely, but this doesn't mean I don't forgive. I've had to realize that I forgive not for the perpetrator, but for my daughters to heal, for me to heal, and for all of us to go on and live our lives without fear and hatred being the defining details. The story of Angela's murder and her murderer will always be a part of our story, a part of my daughters' childhood, but I forgive, so that it is not the main plot of our life story, and so that we can go on to write new stories, better stories, happier stories.

Growing Through Forgiveness

When I am hurt, when I am in pain, when I am angry with someone for what they have done to me, I know the only way to end these feelings is to accept them. I know that the only way out of these feelings is to go through them. We get into all sorts of trouble when we try to find a way to circumvent this natural process. Growth happens through obstacles and only with resistance. A tree must push up against the dirt, the solid resistance of the ground, in order to grow. Muscles grow when we apply a counterforce of resistance against them, but first they tear apart and break down, only to become even stronger in the rebuilding. A butterfly struggles against the cocoon that surrounds it, and it is this very struggling that makes it resilient enough to survive when it breaks free. So it is that you and I must struggle through our anger, grief, and sadness, and push against the pain and suffering on our way to forgiving. When we don't forgive, there is a part of us that doesn't grow as it should. Like the butterfly, we must become stronger and more resilient, and we will transform. We cannot remain frozen in a chrysalis.

We would understand if the Dalai Lama, after more than fifty years in exile, was embittered and full of hate for the people responsible for his and his people's exile, but instead he has made the choice to forgive, and he is one of the most joyful and compassionate people I have ever met. We admire people like this, people who grow through forgiving. His compassion is all the more remarkable because of the forces set against him, which could have evoked anger and rage. We can all strive to be this way. But it does not come easy or cheap. We must choose forgiveness over and over again, and cultivate it as a quality of our character.

Sometimes we are able to forgive quickly and sometimes more slowly. If you find that you are still resistant to the idea of forgiving, it is understandable. Many people will carry grudges and resentments for years, believing this will somehow hurt the other person. In truth, it often only hurts the one who carries the grudge or resentment. Many of us live our lives believing that hating the person who hurt us will somehow end the anguish, that destroying others will fix our broken, aching places. It does not. So many seek this path and it is only when they stand in the aftermath of destruction, amid the rubble of hatred, that they realize the pain is still there. The loss is still there. Forgiving is the only thing that can transform the aching wounds and the searing pain of loss. In the next chapter, we will move on to the final step of the Fourfold Path, renewing or releasing our relationship with the person who has hurt us.

But first, let us pause to listen to what the heart hears.

I can draw you as a cypher
So unlike me
I can make you less than human
I can erase your story
Then I will have no work to do
And nothing to forgive
But there is this pile of pain waiting for me
And I cannot remove it without facing your story
There is a pile of pain waiting for me
And to clear it away
I must admit our common humanity

Summary
Granting Forgiveness

- Forgiveness is a choice.
- We grow through forgiving.
- Forgiving is how we move from victim to hero in our story.
- We know we are healing when we are able to tell a new story.

Meditation

Loving Kindness

1. Close your eyes. Imagine an emotion that makes you feel good. It can be love or kindness or compassion or gratitude or all of these emotions.

2. Allow this emotion or combination of emotions to radiate out from inside you. This is what it feels like to be free of fear, anger, hatred, and resentment. This place of peace lives within you always and belongs to you. You can step into this place whenever you wish. It is yours, and no one can take it from you.

3. Now imagine the person or people you are trying to forgive. Imagine that you are their mother and they are like a tiny baby in your arms, before they hurt you, before they hurt anyone. See their goodness and humanity.

4. Can you bless them and wish them well? Can you send them compassion and kindness? Can you let them go?

Stone Ritual

Washing the Stone

1. Take your stone, which has been with you through this journey along the path. You have spoken to it, you have clenched it, and now you will cleanse it.
2. Get a bowl of water or go to a body of water. Dip your stone in the water three times. Each time you dip the stone, say "I forgive you."

Readers may also wish to perform the following additional ritual as part of their healing along the Fourfold Path:

Sand and Stone

1. You will need a sandy place where there are stones available.
2. What do you want to forgive? With your finger or a stick, write that hurt in the sand.
3. What are three attributes of the person you want to forgive that you value or treasure? With a marker or a pencil, write these on a stone.
4. What is written in sand will soon be gone. What is written on stone endures.

Journal Exercise

1. Begin by writing down a story of the person who harmed you. What do you know about this person? If you do not know them, what can you find out about them? What do you have in common? In what ways are you similar?
2. What have you lost by not being able to forgive? Has this inability to forgive harmed you and the ones you love?
3. Now write down how this painful experience has actually made you stronger. How has it helped you grow and have empathy for others? How has it ennobled you?
4. Finally, write your story again but this time not as the victim but as the hero. How did you deal with the situation, how have you grown, and how will you prevent such harm from happening to others?

Chapter 7

Renewing or Releasing the Relationship

I WAS THERE ON A PASTORAL CALL. This was the third time I was visiting this man on a pastoral call.

The first time had started well enough. In March 1988 PW Botha, the man known as die Groot Krokodil (the Great Crocodile), was the state president of South Africa and I was the Anglican archbishop of Cape Town, coming to him to plead for mercy. Five men and one woman were two short days away from the hangman's noose. The Sharpeville Six had been condemned to death. I had come to plead for their lives. Botha made no promises but offered a glimmer of hope. He would be willing to consider extenuating circumstances and might offer a stay of execution. After that, the meeting made a sharp turn and headed downhill. Botha became annoyed by this petition from me and other church leaders. He began to upbraid me in his trademark finger-wagging style. I responded in kind: "I am not a small boy! Don't think you are talking to a small boy!" The meeting descended to accusations and counteraccusations, and I stormed out of his office in a rage. Not my finest hour!

Almost a decade later, I again stood in his house. It was my second pastoral call on him and the first time I had met him since I had stormed out of his office all those years ago. He was no longer state president. Nelson Mandela was our head of state. I was the chairperson of the Truth and Reconciliation Commission, and I had come to him with a message from the former prisoner who was now our inspirational leader. Come and testify before the commission. "Mandela will sit beside you while you give your testimony," I assured him. The octogenarian Botha declined.

The third and final pastoral call transpired a few weeks later. Botha's wife, Eliza, had died. I came as a loving husband to stand beside another loving husband in his grief.

We shared a long history, he and I. Over these many years our relationship had changed and changed again. We had been adversaries. We had been supplicant and grantor. We had been judge and accused. Between our meetings a Fourfold Path of forgiveness had unfolded. We were two men who had learned to renew our relationship again and again. I had forgiven him for the injuries of years past. We were in a new relationship. Now we were just two South African men.

Forgiveness is not the end of the Fourfold Path, because the granting of forgiveness is not the end of the process of healing. We all live in a delicate web of community, visible and invisible, and time and again the connecting threads get damaged and must be repaired. Once you have been able to forgive, the final step is to either renew or release the relationship you have with the one who has harmed you. Indeed, even if you never speak to the person again, even if you never see them again, even if they are dead, they live on in ways that affect your life profoundly. To finish the forgiveness journey and create the wholeness and peace you crave, you must choose whether to renew or release the relationship. After this final step in the Fourfold Path, you wipe the slate clean of all that caused a breach in the past. No more debts are owed. No more resentments fester. Only when you renew or release the relationship can you have a future unfettered by the past.

Renewing or Releasing

What does it mean to renew or release a relationship? You might think you are not in a relationship with the stranger who assaulted you or the person in prison who killed your loved one or the cheating spouse you divorced so many years ago, but a relationship is created and maintained by the very act of harm that stands between you. This relationship, like every relationship that calls for forgiveness, must be either renewed or released. When your spouse says, for example, "I'm sorry for yelling at you," you may forgive and continue on in the marriage, renewing the relationship. When a boyfriend or girlfriend says, "I'm sorry for betraying your trust," you may forgive but choose not to see that person again, instead releasing the relationship.

The decision to renew or release is a personal choice that only you can make. Obviously it is easier to choose to renew a relationship when it is a close connection, such as a spouse, parent, sibling, or close friend. With these intimates it is much harder to release the relationship completely, as the threads of memory and intimacy that bind you are strong. It is easier to release a relationship with an acquaintance, neighbor, or stranger, because these people often do not hold as much of your heart.

The considered decision to release a relationship is a valid choice. Even so, the preference is always toward renewal or reconciliation, except in cases where safety is an issue. When we choose to release a relationship, that person walks off with a piece of our hearts and a piece of our history. The choice is not one to be made lightly or in the heat of the moment.

Renewing our relationships is how we harvest the fruits that forgiveness has planted. Renewal is not an act of restoration. We do not make a carbon copy of the relationship we had before the hurt or insult. Renewing a relationship is a creative act. We make a new relationship. It is possible to build a new relationship regardless of the realities of the old relationship. It is even possible to renew a relationship born out of violence, as was the case with Linda Biehl, Easy Nofemela, and Ntobeko Peni.

As we briefly touched on in chapter 3, Linda Biehl is the mother of Amy Biehl, a Stanford University student who, in 1992, won a Fulbright scholarship and decided to go to South Africa to work in the struggle to end apartheid. On August 25, 1993, she was driving into the Gugulethu township when her car was stopped by an angry mob. The group had just emerged from a political meeting to protest the police slaying of a young black boy. Amy's passion for justice and her purpose for being in South Africa were not written on her face. To the protesters, Amy was just another white person, another symbol of apartheid oppression. They dragged her from the vehicle and beat, stoned, and stabbed her to death. Amy was twenty-six years old.

In 1998, the four young men convicted of her murder were granted amnesty by the TRC. Amy's parents, Linda and Peter Biehl, not only supported this decision but went on to establish the Amy Biehl Foundation Trust in Cape Town. It is a charity dedicated to fighting violence and helping the very community where Amy was murdered. Two of the men, Easy Nofemela and Ntobeko Peni, now work for the foundation named after the woman they killed. They have a close relationship with Linda Biehl (Peter Biehl has since passed away) and have formed a unique bond.

How does this happen? How is it possible to renew a relationship born out of such pain and grief? While each person and circumstance is different, what seems to be most true in stories like those of the Biehl family is the desire to create meaning out of suffering and to move forward and heal after a tragedy. It is what makes us human, this need to fix what is broken, repair relationships, and find understanding and a larger purpose after we have lost something or someone dear to us. It was not easy for the Biehls to face the men who murdered their daughter. It was not easy for the perpetrators to face the truth of what they'd done. But through reconciliation, all were empowered to grow and move forward, to heal and unite in a common purpose.

Their story is transformed by their reconciliation. It is not a story of how one woman was violently attacked by a group of strangers. It is now a story about South Africa's struggle for democracy as well as a powerful, inspiring story about the beauty and goodness that emerges from forgiveness and reconciliation. The Biehls needed to understand the circumstances of their daughter's death, and in seeking that understanding, they were able to find a larger understanding of the politics and the people involved. Linda says, "I can't look at myself as a victim—it diminishes me as a person. And Easy and Ntobeko don't see themselves as killers. They didn't set out to kill Amy Biehl. But Easy has told me that it's one thing to reconcile what happened as a political activist, quite another to reconcile it in your heart." (We will return to Easy's struggle to seek forgiveness in the next chapter.)

Renewing relationships is how we turn our curses into blessings and continue to grow through our forgiving. It is how we make restitution for what was taken and set right what was made wrong. Even if the relationship was injurious or hurtful, it is still a piece of shared history. Ubuntu says, "I am incomplete without you," and whenever possible we must do the hard work to rebuild right relations with one another. Enemies can become friends, and perpetrators can recover their lost humanity.

I Have a Part

A very important but difficult piece of renewing relationships is accepting responsibility for our part in any conflict. If we have a relationship in need of repair, we must remember that the wrong is not usually all on one side, and we are more easily able to restore relations when we look at our contribution to a conflict.

There are times when we truly did nothing, as when a stranger robs us, but even then we have a role in permitting or participating in a society where such desperation exists. I do not say this to inspire guilt or apportion blame, since no one person creates a society. But each of us does have a role in the society we have created. We can take responsibility for our part in a way that frees us from being a victim and allows us to open our hearts. We are always at our best when compassion enables us to recognize the unique pressures and singular stories of the people on the other side of our conflicts. This is true for any conflict, from a personal spat to an international dispute.

Ubuntu says that we all have a part in creating a society that creates a perpetrator; therefore, I have a part not only in every conflict I may find myself in personally, but in every conflict happening right now in my family, in my community, in my nation, and around the globe. This thought may seem overwhelming. The gift hidden in the challenge of Ubuntu is that we don't need to walk the corridors of power to build peace. Each of us can create a more peaceful world from wherever in the world we each stand.

Asking for What You Need

How do we genuinely renew or release a relationship after we have been hurt? How do we move forward and heal from the loss? In order to renew or release the relationship, we must make meaning of our experiences. This is how we continue to move away from our identity as victims. If your best friend calls you an ugly name, you would perhaps want an apology and an explanation before you renew the relationship. When we are hurt, we most often need the truth of why we were hurt—why a person we trusted lied to us, or a spouse was unfaithful, or a stranger saw fit to accost us. Often it is this truth-telling that gives us the momentum we need to complete the final step in the Fourfold Path.

We may also claim restitution or recompense for what was taken or lost. If your neighbor steals from you, you would want to have the item returned before you renew your relationship as neighbors.

Ask yourself what you need to renew or release a relationship, and then, if you can, ask it of the person who harmed you. Your decision to renew or release may very well hinge on whether you get what you need. You may need that person to listen to your story and hear the hurt you have experienced. You may need to know the perpetrator is remorseful before you renew the relationship, and be assured that it won't happen again. If the person is not sorry for what they have done, you may decide it is best to release the relationship.

If it is not possible to speak directly to the person who harmed you and ask of them what you need, ask it of others. Ask for empathy. Ask for belief. Ask for understanding or the space to tell your story, and name your hurt until you are done. When you ask for what you need to heal, you are no longer a victim without any say in your fate. And ultimately, whether you get what you need totally or even partially, this does not determine whether you can renew the relationship.

I was not able to ask my father for the explanation and apology I wanted before he died, but this does not mean I let go of the relationship. I was able to renew the relationship with him in my heart, and sometimes that is all we can do, but doing it makes all the difference.

An Unusual Request

When Dan and Lynn Wagner received a letter from the parole office letting them know that Lisa—the woman who had killed their two daughters in a car accident—was being released from prison, they knew that in order to continue healing they had to set up a meeting with her on their terms. Dan says their plan was to release the relationship and close the final chapter in their story:

> We called the parole officer and asked if he could set up a meeting between Lisa and us. We explained that we had never gone to court because she had pled guilty, and therefore we had never actually met her. The parole officer said it was an unusual request, and that meeting with us was against Lisa's conditions of parole. His superiors, however, approved it and we set a date.
>
> We really didn't discuss what we were going to say to her. We just wanted to get this meeting over with and get that last door closed. We knew from the moment she was sentenced to prison that the day would eventually come when we'd meet her, and we wanted that first meeting to be in a controlled environment like this, not in the checkout line at some grocery store.
>
> When we walked into the meeting room and laid our eyes on Lisa for the first time, we both hugged her. I don't

know why, but it suddenly seemed as if we had all been through this war together. When I hugged her, I started crying and couldn't stop and couldn't let go. In that hug and in my heart I felt a sense of relief. After seven years, I was finally meeting the woman who had killed my daughters. But I felt no anger, no hatred—just relief. So I cried.

We eventually sat down around a large table. Lisa spoke about her twelve-step recovery process and that step nine, Making Amends, would be for her a "living amends." Lynn asked her to clarify what she meant by that. Lisa said she wanted to share her experience with others in hopes she could prevent others from taking a life as she had taken the lives of Mandie and Carrie.

We thanked her for pleading guilty and keeping us out of the court proceedings. She kept saying, "I *was* guilty." Then the parole office said he had never seen anything like this and perhaps we are all serving a God of reconciliation.

We walked into that building in fear, thinking we were finally going to have an end. But it turned out to be a new beginning. Lynn and Lisa have since been invited to speak together, and they go to jails and churches and universities and share our story. It's funny how it's our story now. And our story has touched a lot of lives. It's about tragedy, yes, but it's also about forgiveness and something someone told me in the early days after the accident: God does not waste his children's pain.

What Is Releasing?

There are times when renewing is not possible. Renewing the relationship might harm you further, or you do not know who harmed you, or the person has died and is not someone you carry in your heart. These are all times when the only option is releasing the relationship, and this too is essential for the completion of your healing journey.

Releasing a relationship is how you free yourself from victimhood and trauma. You can choose to not have someone in your life any longer, but you have released the relationship only when you have truly chosen that path without wishing that person ill. Releasing is refusing to let an experience or a person occupy space in your head or heart any longer. It is releasing not only the relationship but your old story of the relationship.

What Is Renewing?

Renewing a relationship is not restoring a relationship. We do not go back to where we were before the hurt happened and pretend it never happened. We create a new relationship out of our suffering, one that is often stronger for what we have experienced together. Our renewed relationships are often deeper because we have faced the truth, recognized our shared humanity, and now tell a new story of a relationship transformed.

I'm Not There Yet

As with all four steps on the Fourfold Path, sometimes you move quickly in one phase and slowly in another. Sometimes you straddle two places at once or you just need more time before moving through the process. If you are not yet ready to either renew or release the relationship with the person who harmed you, this is okay. If you do not yet know what you need to ask of that person in order to heal, this is also okay. We don't complete this last step—or any step in the Fourfold Path—from our heads, but rather from our hearts. And it can take time to know what's truly in our hearts.

For Mpho, she is not yet sure whether she wishes to renew or release the relationship with the man accused of Angela's murder. Like me, her preference is always for renewal, but it is often difficult.

I still have this incredible sadness. We all do. Do I want to renew the relationship? Do I want to release the relationship? I don't know. The truth is, I'm not there yet.

I have forgiven him. He is another human being and he has a story too. It's our story now. And Angela's story. And her family's story. There are so many individual stories, but we share this one story. That's the biggest difference I've seen in this forgiveness process. It's gone from "my story" to "our story." It's no longer about my pain, but our pain. There is a comfort in that, a solace.

Intellectually, I have forgiven him, and I know this because I have no desire to exact retribution, nor do I wish him ill. He does not owe me anything. Emotionally, I'm not quite there yet, because it still hurts, and I know there is still healing work to be done.

If he did kill her, it would help move things along more quickly if I could know why he did what he did. I want to know what he was thinking and why he couldn't have asked for help for whatever he was going through. Whatever it was, why couldn't he have come to me? Why did Angela have to pay such a price? How was her life worth so little to him?

I think I would also need to know that what he did matters to him. I would need to know that he wrestles with the fact that he took a life. I would want to know if his soul hurts and he is pained by what he has been accused of doing. It won't change anything, but it will help me understand. I would want to understand him so that I can know what we need to do differently, so that no one gets to such a place of desperation that a thing becomes more important than a life.

I can't speak to him because of the criminal proceedings, but if I could, I would tell him that I don't have the words to say just how sad I am. I would say, "Look what has happened to us."

As Mpho shares her journey of forgiveness, I am reminded that what happens to me also happens to us. We are all in a relationship with one another, and when that relationship breaks, we all have the responsibility to roll up our sleeves and get to the hard work of repair. Apology and forgiveness are wonderful tools to repair what has been broken. Renew your relationships when you can and release them when you can't. When we practice this last step of the Fourfold Path, we keep anger, resentment, hatred, and despair from ever having the last word.

We all get hurt and we all inflict hurt. If you are in need of forgiveness, the Fourfold Path is also for you. In the next chapter, we will look at the Fourfold Path for those times when you are the one in need of forgiveness.

But first, let us pause and listen to what the heart hears.

We cannot begin again
We cannot make a new start as though the past has not passed
But we can plant something new
In the burnt ground
In time we will harvest a new story of who we are
We will
Build a relationship that is tempered by the fire of our history
You are a person who has hurt me
I am a person who could hurt you
And knowing those truths we choose to make something new
Forgiveness is my back bent to clear away the dead tangle of hurt
and recrimination
And make a space, a field fit for planting
When I stand to survey this place I can choose to invite
you in to sow seeds for a different harvest
Or I can choose to let you go
And let that field lie fallow

Summary
Renewing or Releasing the Relationship

- The preference is always to renew unless there is a question of safety.
- Ask for what you need from the perpetrator in order to renew or release the relationship.
- You may need an apology, an explanation, a tangible object, or to never see that person again.
- Look at your part in any conflict.
- When you renew a relationship, it is stronger for what you have been through, but it is always different.
- By renewing or releasing a relationship you free yourself from victimhood and trauma.

Meditation

Releasing or Renewing

1. Enter your place of safety.
2. Invite your trusted and affirming companion to sit with you.
3. Allow yourself to feel all the hope and any anxiety that surrounds your relationship with the person you have forgiven.
4. Describe your hopes and fears to your companion.
5. Your companion will not judge your hopes, your fears, or your decisions. Your companion will affirm your inner wisdom.
6. When you feel settled in your choices, you can leave this space.

Stone Ritual

Renewing or Releasing the Stone

1. Decide whether you will turn your stone into a new thing of beauty or release it back into nature.
2. If you have chosen to renew the stone, decide how you will paint it or decorate it. You may also choose to turn it into something useful in your home or garden.
3. If you have chosen to release your stone, you may take it back to the place you found it and set it down, or you may take it to a new place that is meaningful to you.
4. Nothing is wasted. Everything, even a stone, has its purpose.

Readers may also wish to perform the following additional ritual as part of their healing along the Fourfold Path:

Make Something Beautiful

1. You will need some art supplies (glue, paint, colored paper, markers, fabric).
2. You will also need a bag.
3. You will complete this exercise using something you consider beautiful and breakable, such as a cup, plate, or tile. (If you cannot use a breakable item, substitute a picture from a magazine, a photograph, or a piece of patterned fabric.)

4. Place the breakable item inside the bag and use your stone to smash the item. (If using a photograph or picture, then use your stone to scrape, scratch, or tear it.)
5. Now use the resulting shards or shreds and your supplies to make something beautiful.

Journal Exercise

1. Was it possible to make something beautiful from what you had?
2. How difficult was it to do so?
3. How closely did your new creation resemble the item you damaged?
4. Could it serve the same function as the original?
5. What did you learn about renewing and releasing as you engaged in this exercise?

Part Three

ALL CAN
BE FORGIVEN

Chapter 8

Needing Forgiveness

"YES, SIR. RIGHT THIS WAY, MADAM," the policeman responded to our query. My wife, Leah, and I knew exactly where we were going. We had no need to ask directions of this fresh-faced London bobby so eager to help us. But after the rudeness and harassment we had come to expect as our due at the hands of the police in our native South Africa, these encounters with English policemen were a sublime pleasure. Police in South Africa were the frontline agents of the apartheid state. Their role was to enforce every indignity in the racist arsenal. So it was quite a shock when we landed in England and found the London bobbies so polite and eager to help us.

Our time in England was in so many ways a haven of civility and hospitality. It was an oasis from the constant prejudice, chaos, and violence we had come to know at home.

For four years we were able to eat in any restaurant, go to any theater, and board any bus. It was liberating and life changing to experience. And then the call came.

Leah and I talked about what it would mean to go back to South Africa after this second period in England. The first time around I had come as a student. This time I had worked for three years for the World Council of Churches in the Theological Education Fund. The children, older now, would have to go back to boarding schools across the border in Swaziland. I could see how much Leah dreaded breaking up our family. I could see how much she dreaded the return to second-class status. But I felt drawn to this new role. I would become the dean of Johannesburg, the senior resident cleric at St. Mary's Cathedral where I had been ordained. I would be the first black person to fill that role. I pressed. Leah has always supported my ministry. She, reluctantly, agreed. It was one of the times that most strained our marriage.

At home in South Africa, in the face of the viciousness of apartheid, I could not be silent. And then the death threats came. I would see Leah or one of the children slowly hang up the phone with a distant look of fear on her face and I knew that it had been another one of those vile threatening calls. I asked Leah then if I should stop speaking up. Quite incredibly, she said to me that she would be happier with me on Robben Island, where Mandela and so many other anti-apartheid stalwarts were imprisoned, than silent outside. This emboldened me more than I can say. But each time I saw her or one of our children shaking in rage or fear after answering one of those phone calls, I knew my actions were the cause of their pain.

We make choices that affect others even when we do not mean to hurt them. Many years later I asked Leah whether she would forgive me for the impact my work had had on her and our family. She smiled at me, perhaps grateful for the acknowledgment of her sacrifice. "I forgave you a long time ago."

From whom do you need forgiveness? What have you done? Have you hurt someone you love? Does the guilt or shame gnaw at you? Have you caused pain and anguish? Are you trapped in the wreckage of your actions with no visible means of escape?

The simple truth is we all make mistakes, and we all need forgiveness. There is no magic wand we can wave to go back in time and change what has happened or undo the harm that has been done, but we can do everything in our power to set right what has been made wrong. We can endeavor to make sure the harm never happens again.

We all need forgiveness. There are times when all of us have been thoughtless or selfish or cruel. As we have said earlier, no act is unforgivable; no person is beyond redemption. Yet, it is not easy to admit one's wrongdoing and ask for forgiveness. "I am sorry" are perhaps the three hardest words to say. We can come up with all manner of justifications to excuse what we have done. When we are willing to let down our defenses and look honestly at our actions, we find there is a great freedom in asking for forgiveness and great strength in admitting the wrong. It is how we free ourselves from our past errors. It is how we are able to move forward into our future, unfettered by the mistakes we have made.

Seeking Forgiveness

We assume it is hard for the person being asked to forgive. It may be harder still for the person seeking forgiveness. Why do we reckon it is easier to be contrite than to be forgiving? It is not. When we have done wrong and seek to make it right, we show the depth of our humanity. We reveal the depth of our desire to heal ourselves. We show the depth of desire to heal those we have harmed.

Stefaans Coetzee traveled the Fourfold Path from Pretoria Central Prison. On Christmas Eve 1996, when he was seventeen, Stefaans and a trio of members of the white supremacist Afrikaner Weerstandsbewegining (AWB) planted a series of bombs in a shopping center in Worcester, South Africa. Their target was a venue frequented by the black population of the city. Their goal was to exact the maximum death toll. Only one of the bombs exploded, but it injured sixty-seven people and left four dead. Three of those who died were children. Shortly after the incident, Coetzee expressed his disappointment at the low death toll.

It was a fellow prisoner who set Coetzee on the healing journey. Eugene de Kock, nicknamed "Prime Evil" by the media for his role in numerous apartheid-era murders, became Coetzee's mentor. "Unless you seek forgiveness from those you have harmed, you will find that you are bound inside two prisons—the one you are in physically and the one you have around your heart. It is never too late to repair the harm you have caused. Then, even though you are behind bars, you will still be free. No one can lock away your ability to change. No one can lock away your goodness or your humanity." On Reconciliation Day in December

2011 a letter from Stefaans was read to a gathering of the surviving victims of the Worcester bombing. In the letter, Stefaans expressed his remorse and asked for forgiveness. Many have forgiven him for his horrific act. Indeed some of the surviving victims of the bombing have visited him in jail. Some have not yet been able to forgive. Stefaans understands that he cannot demand forgiveness, but he describes being forgiven as "a grace . . . that resulted in freedom beyond understanding."

When I harm another, whether intentionally or not, I inevitably harm myself. I become less than I am meant to be. I become less than I am capable of being. When I harm another, I need to restore what I have taken from that person. Or make a gesture of recompense. I need to restore what I have lost within myself through my harmful words or actions.

To recover what has been lost requires that we take an honest look at ourselves and confront our past mistakes. It requires that we admit what we have done and take responsibility for our actions. It requires a genuine remorse, which comes from understanding how our wrongs have affected others. It requires that we look into our own souls and realize that a person who hurts another is not the person we wish to be. It requires that we be willing to make amends and to do whatever is required to repair the relationship, even if this means never seeing the other person again. We must be willing to respect our own progress along the Fourfold Path. We must be willing to respect that the one whose forgiveness we seek must make his or her own journey along the Fourfold Path. We cannot dictate that person's pace or progress. Even

if we never find the forgiveness we seek, we make the courageous choice to walk this path because we must make every
effort possible to do the right thing.

Never Walking the Fourfold Path

Few of us are ever in a mad rush to acknowledge our harmful actions. But if the process of forgiveness is to succeed, we
must accept responsibility for what we have done. We must
be able to state the truth of what we have done in order to
heal the breech in a relationship. We must tell the truth in
order to heal the places inside us that break when we hurt
another. Kelly Connor was not able to talk about what she
did. She was not able to engage in a process that would lead
to healing, and it ended up affecting her life in ways she
could never have imagined.

When Kelly was seventeen, she asked her dad to drive
her to her job in Perth, Australia, as she normally didn't get
to drive herself. "He wanted to have a lie-in, so he said no.
I was so excited to drive myself in his car. It was my sister
Jayne's twelfth birthday. We were going to celebrate later
that day. I was going on holiday with my friends in a few
weeks. Life was wonderful. I was happy. I had so much to
look forward to."

On the way to work that day, Kelly accidentally hit and
killed seventy-year-old Margaret Healy as she was crossing
the street:

> I was going too fast up a hill and looking in my rearview
> mirror. I crested the hill and I didn't see her until it was too
> late. I remember her look of horror. She was old, but she

tried to run. She was fighting for her life. I didn't set out to kill her, but I took her life. It was an accident, yes, but I was responsible. I was at fault, but the police wouldn't let me tell the true story of what happened.

"How fast were you going?" the policeman asked.

"I'm not sure but probably around forty-five miles per hour. I was going too fast."

"Do you know the speed limit?" the policeman asked.

"Thirty-five miles per hour."

"Then how fast were you going?" he asked again.

"Probably forty-five miles per hour," I repeated, confused.

He sighed, asking again, "What is the speed limit?"

"Thirty-five miles per hour."

"Then how fast were you traveling?"

"I didn't know what to say. Were they asking me to lie?

"Thirty-five miles per hour?" I finally said.

"Good," he said, typing up the answer that would not lead to my prosecution.

My mother passed an edict that same night that said we had to live our lives as if this never happened and told me I was forbidden to ever speak of it again. Ever. My name was in the paper, but I couldn't mention my shame, my fear. I lived in terror and anxiety for years, believing the police were going to come and take me away to the cells. When I slept, I had nightmares where demons and angels did battle for my soul. I was confused about how to go on living, why I should be allowed to go on living. I felt completely alone and completely lost, disconnected from the world around me and cast out by all who were supposed to love me. I didn't think I was worthy of having a life because I had taken a life. There was no safe place or safe person to speak to about how I felt. It seemed as if there was no room in the world for a young girl who had done what I did and felt as I felt. Shame, dread, pain, guilt. I know my father also felt guilty for not driving me that day, but we could not speak of it. My family fell apart. My father ended up leaving home four months after the accident and vanishing. He died ten years later. I never saw him again. I never got to say good-bye to him. My entire family died the day I hit Margaret. My friendships died. My joy died. My childhood and my future both died. I wished I had died.

I couldn't ask for forgiveness nor could I forgive myself. Nobody knew the truth of what happened. The police and the courts would not punish me, so I punished myself. I never formed any close relationships because I had this secret. If I became close to anyone, I moved to a new town because I was so afraid they would find out, and I couldn't bear the pain of keeping my secret and living my lie. I tried to commit suicide because I believed the only person I could talk to about what happened, the only person who could forgive me, was the woman I killed. I was locked up in a psychiatric hospital, and even there I still couldn't tell anyone my feelings or the truth about what happened. I kept my shame and my secrets locked inside me for decades.

It took Kelly thirty years to admit the wrong and break the silence imposed by her mother on that tragic day. Once she was finally able to admit the wrong, she was able to make space for her own anguish, ask for forgiveness, and finally, three decades and much suffering later, release the relationship. Today Kelly lives in London and speaks publicly about the accident. She has also written a book, *To Cause a Death,* about her journey from silence to self-forgiveness. Her life was forever altered not only by taking a life, but by her inability to walk her own Fourfold Path of forgiveness and self-forgiveness. "It would have been better," she says, "if I could have gone to prison. I might actually have had a chance. My family might have had a chance. But by locking up all the secrets and the guilt and the shame, instead of locking me up, I never had a chance to make it right. I never had a chance to really be free."

One: Admitting the Wrong

Ideally, the Fourfold Path begins with the one who has inflicted the harm admitting what they have done. When we are able to admit what we have done wrong, we begin the process of receiving forgiveness on sure footing. It makes it easier for the one we have harmed to forgive us. There is no guarantee that they will forgive us, but by walking the Fourfold Path we create a better chance for forgiveness. Even if there is little hope that the one we have wounded will forgive, we can still walk the Fourfold Path for our own healing. The person who grants forgiveness receives a gift. The person who asks forgiveness receives the healing gift of an honest reckoning. When we seek forgiveness, we hope that our humble admission will help the person we have harmed. We hope that our contrition will heal the relationship we have impaired, so we set out bravely. Even though we are uncertain of the outcome, we know this journey is our only hope for freedom and wholeness.

This first step can be difficult. It is not easy to admit our wrongs. But it must be done. As Kelly learned, it is much more difficult to live a lie. It is a burden to carry our secrets and our shame, our guilt and our remorse. Often the fear of telling the person what we have done is much greater than the reaction we will get from actually admitting the wrong.

Note

You may wish to gather support as you embark on the process of admitting a wrong. It can be helpful to practice what you are going to say with a friend, family member, or someone you trust.

Only when we can speak the secrets can we hope to banish our shame and live with truth and integrity.

Admitting the wrong is how we begin to take responsibility for hurting another human being. As we saw time and time again in the TRC, victims often suffer more from not knowing. If we genuinely wish to make things right, we will not compound the initial harm by failing to make an honest confession. It is the first step in truly thinking of another first. When we experience true remorse, then we can make an honest confession and begin to relieve the suffering we have caused. This is true whether we've taken a life, stolen from a neighbor, betrayed a spouse, or done any of a host of other deeds of cruelty or thoughtlessness.

How Do I Admit the Wrong?

The best way to begin anything that feels too difficult is often just to begin. In admitting what we have done, we must do so without any expectations about the response we may get. We stand firmly in our integrity and state the facts of what we've done. "I've stolen your property," we may say, or "I've lied to you." Another crucial piece of admitting what we've done is to acknowledge that it was wrong and affirm we know we have hurt the person, perhaps badly and irreparably.

We also must be willing to answer any and all questions the victim has about what we've done. We may be asked to clarify events, dates, times, and other factual matters. Or we may be asked to explain why we did what we did. We must be careful not to self-justify or excuse our actions in any way. "I was thoughtless and selfish" is a far different answer than "I was angry and not in my right mind." It has a different texture and tenor and will get a far different reaction from the person we have harmed. It may be factually true that we were not in our right mind, but we still must be accountable for every action we take in life that hurts another. There can be no reconciliation without responsibility.

What If My Actions Were Justified?

Perhaps you have hurt someone close to you and you did not intend to do so. Do you still engage in the Fourfold Path if you feel justified by what you've done? Do you engage in the Fourfold Path even if you haven't done anything and the other person is still angry with you for an imagined slight or wrongdoing?

Ubuntu answers yes. Ubuntu places the highest value on whole and healthy relationships. If someone is hurt, Ubuntu enjoins us to try to understand that person's pain. Ubuntu invites us to see from the other person's perspective. We have perhaps all heard the question "Do you want to be right or do you want to be happy?" We all want to be happy, and often that means we apologize and witness the harm another feels we have caused, even if we do not believe that what we did "should" have hurt. In matters of the heart, there is no "should."

If someone is hurting because of us, whether we've intended that hurt or not, we must do whatever we can to make it right. This is as true for little disagreements as it is for larger crimes.

What If the Victim Doesn't Know?

You know your past. Only you know the secrets, the guilt, and the shame you carry. If you do not face up to your past, it will haunt you. If you cannot admit your mistakes or crimes, the guilt or shame is going to rear its ugly head in some destructive way or another. These things have a way of popping up, and often in ways that you cannot control.

We all lose a part of our humanity, of our divinity, when we hurt another human being. And that loss is a heavy burden to carry. Whether the person you have harmed knows it or not, you know it, and that is enough to seek the path to make it right. Though the path to making it right may or may not include telling your story to the person you have injured. Revealing an unknown betrayal may cause a deeper injury to the victim than that person's ignorance of your deed. If this is the case, then you can tell your story to a trusted counselor or confessor.

What If I Am Afraid of the Consequences?

It is understandable that you may be afraid of what might happen when you admit your wrongs. There may be a price to pay. That price will be far cheaper than the personal cost of keeping silent. The weight of guilt can be staggering and the burden of shame unbearable.

If there are legal consequences to consider, you may wish to consult counsel before admitting the wrong. You may also want to bring a trusted third party along to support both you and your victim. This can be a family member, a friend, or a professional. The important thing to remember is that there can be no genuine forgiveness, and therefore no genuine healing, without genuine truth. It is what sets us all free.

Two: Witnessing the Anguish and Apologizing

It is hard to admit our wrongs, to make a full confession of our crimes. It is also hard to witness the harm we have caused and to apologize. Witnessing and apologizing calls for a humility that does not come easily. Even when we know we have been thoughtless or selfish or cruel, it is still not easy to admit it, face the hurt we have caused, and say the words "I am sorry." Truth be told, those three words often feel like the hardest words to say to another human being. Those three little words can die in our mouths a hundred times before we can say them. It is worth practicing the words "I am sorry" when we commit small slights because in time we will all need them for the large hurts.

When we witness the anguish we have caused another, we help that person heal, and we help the relationship heal. Victims need to tell their stories. Victims need to express how much they have been hurt. And as perpetrators, we need to be fearless enough to stand in front of those we have hurt and open our hearts to make space for their pain. We had a part in creating it, and we have a part in healing it.

How Do I Witness the Anguish?

Victims need to feel they are being heard and affirmed. The best way to do this is to not argue the facts of their stories or the ways they are hurting. If your spouse says you lied last Wednesday, and you lied to them last Thursday, it will not help rebuild the trust by arguing the date of the offense. If your child says "You did not show up to my football game, and you are never there for me," it does not serve a healing purpose for you to counter with all the other football games you have attended as irrefutable proof you are there for your child.

When people are hurting, they cannot be cross-examined out of their pain. We all want our pain to be acknowledged and understood. We all want to feel safe to express our hurt feelings in all their various forms and textures. If you argue with the person you have harmed, that person will not feel safe, nor will that person feel understood. When someone is hurt, that person wants his or her pain to be understood and validated. Without that understanding, the forgiveness process will stall and you will both remain trapped in an endless loop of telling the story and naming the hurt. Empathy is the gateway to forgiveness for you and for the one you have harmed.

There are no prescribed words to witnessing the anguish. There is no rehearsal process you can go through. You need to be open and have a genuine desire to heal the harm you have caused. If your victim has questions, answer them honestly and thoroughly. Speak from your heart. If that person asks how you could have done what you did, tell the truth. Be careful not to excuse or justify your actions.

It is truly a painful step in the forgiveness process to face the ripple effects of the harm we have caused. As we saw in Mpho's story of Angela's murder, Angela and her family

Witnessing the Anguish

- Do not argue.
- Do not cross-examine.
- Listen and acknowledge the harm you have caused.
- Do not justify your actions or your motivations.
- Answer all questions honestly and thoroughly.

were not the only ones affected by the violence. The violence affected Mpho, her children, my grandchildren's school friends, and the sense of safety of all the people in our community. The violence was done to Angela, but the pain was widespread. We are all so very interconnected that when we hurt one person, the pain often ripples far deeper and wider than we can ever imagine. By witnessing the anguish from injuries we have caused, we begin to turn back the tide of harm. And by following up with a sincere apology, we stem the flow of future damage.

Three Simple Words

After we admit our wrongs and witness the anguish, we must offer a genuine apology. There is something magical about saying "I am sorry." There is healing in the very utterance. Who among us has not had to say these words and who among us has not wished to hear them? "I am sorry" can be a bridge between nations, spouses, friends, and enemies. A whole world can be built on the very foundation laid out in these three simple words: "I am sorry."

If we neglect this important step, we can create cracks in the foundation of our forgiving.

We may need to utter those magical words many times before they are heard and felt. We may have to say them many times before they are believed. What is important is that we are courageous enough to say them, vulnerable enough to mean them, and humble enough to repeat them as many times as necessary.

How Do I Apologize?

When you apologize, you are restoring the dignity that you have violated in the person you have hurt. You are also acknowledging that the offense has happened. You are taking responsibility for your part in causing harm. When you apologize with humility and with true remorse for hurting another, you open a space for healing.

We have all heard children mutter "Sorry" when forced to do so by a scolding parent, and we have also all heard the bitter resentment in the child's utterance. A hollow or insincere apology can only compound the initial damage done. An apology offered as a way to get out of trouble or to placate an upset person is no apology at all. When you apologize, do it from the heart. If you do not feel it, do not say it. It is only when we recognize the suffering of the other person, and the true harm we have caused, that our apologies will be genuine. If we are truly remorseful, our apologies will come wholeheartedly, not reluctantly. When we acknowledge and admit our wrongs, freely and willingly face the pain we have caused, and truly feel remorse for our behavior, our apologies will leave us feeling as if a huge weight has been lifted off our shoulders. Even when our apologies are restorative, when we are driven by Ubuntu to repair a breach of which we were unaware, those apologies must be genuine to be healing.

What If I Can't Apologize Directly to the Person I Have Harmed?

The freedom and healing that comes from saying "I'm sorry" is still possible even if the person to whom you need to apologize is no longer alive or there is no possible way to speak to them directly. You can write them a letter that you bury or burn. You can also participate in a number of online anonymous apology websites or even call an apology hotline phone number and leave your apology as an anonymous voicemail message.

That these outlets for apology exist is a testament to the healing power of an apology offered. Ideally, we could all face our accusers and express our remorse and offer our apologies straightforwardly. This ideal is not always possible, but we can still engage in this step along the Fourfold Path.

Three: Asking for Forgiveness

We often wonder if it is selfish to ask for forgiveness. Are we asking to be let off the hook, to not pay our debts to society, or to not be held accountable for our actions? It is not selfish to ask for forgiveness, and in truth it is the highest form of accountability. By asking for forgiveness, we are committing ourselves to the possibility of change. We are signing up for the hard work of transformation. None of us is irredeemable, and to dismiss any of us as unworthy of forgiveness is to dismiss all of us.

We ask for forgiveness because none of us can live in the past. The victim cannot live in the past. The perpetrator cannot live in the past. When we ask for forgiveness, we ask

Anonymous Apology Websites

www.perfectapology.com
www.imsorry.com
www.joeapology.com

Apology Hotline Number (in the United States)

(347) 201-2446

for permission to begin again. When we ask for forgiveness, we ask to no longer be held hostage by the past. When we ask for forgiveness, we are in the middle of a profound process that sets both victim and perpetrator free. There is no asking for forgiveness without admitting the wrong and witnessing the anguish.

If you still find it hard to ask for forgiveness, there may be some work on self-forgiveness to do, which we will discuss in chapter 9. Asking for forgiveness from your victims is another way of acknowledging your responsibility and your sincere wish to repair what you have broken. There is no guarantee you will be forgiven, and there is no guarantee that a relationship will be restored. But through the asking we do our part, and it is only when we do everything in our power and walk the path of forgiving to the best of our ability that we liberate ourselves from a shameful past. Every sinner has the potential to see with the eyes of a saint and recover the humanity he or she has lost through hurtful behavior.

How Do I Ask for Forgiveness?

Asking for forgiveness is so much more than saying the words "Will you forgive me?" When we ask for forgiveness, we express our remorse and offer an apology. We acknowledge the harm and explain why and how we will not hurt the victim again. When we genuinely seek forgiveness, we will do whatever it takes to make things right—we will be willing not only to ask the victim if they will grant us forgiveness but also to offer whatever form of restitution they require in order to forgive. It is as simple and as difficult as that. Neither side in a conflict wishes to be tied forever to the roles of either victim or perpetrator.

In the TRC, it was not a requirement for the perpetrators to express their remorse in order to be granted amnesty. At first the commissioners were outraged by this, but later we came to see the wisdom of this decision. As a commission, we did not want the perpetrators pretending to be sorry or merely offering hollow words and false remorse in order to fulfill a requirement for amnesty. What we were after most was the truth and a way for the victims to be heard and have their questions answered. Although an expression of remorse was not required, almost everyone who came before the commission did, in fact, turn toward their victims to express remorse and regret for their actions, and almost all of those asked for forgiveness.

I was truly humbled by the forgiveness I saw so freely granted. I was awed by the gracious words of apology and profound acts of forgiveness that came out of honest dialogue. There is no script I can write that will express your remorse. You must write your own script directly from your heart and your conscience. This is the place where the power of forgiving and being forgiven is generated. No one can place remorse in another's heart. Either you feel it or you don't. And your victim will know if your remorse is genuine and heartfelt.

When Easy Nofemela first learned of the TRC, he didn't want to give his testimony about the murder of Amy Biehl. But then he read a press report in which Linda and Peter Biehl—Amy's parents—said it was not up to them to forgive but up to the people of South Africa "to learn to forgive."

He made a decision to go before the commission and tell his story and express his remorse. "Amnesty wasn't my motivation. I just wanted to ask for forgiveness. I wanted to say in front of Linda and Peter, face-to-face, 'I am sorry. Can you forgive me?' I wanted to be free in my mind and body."

As we shared in the previous chapter, a new relationship was formed between the Biehls and Easy because he was willing to express his remorse and ask for forgiveness. A new story was written out of the tragedy of Amy's murder, and so much good and so much healing has happened in her name and in her memory.

What If They Will Not Forgive?

There is no assurance that when you ask for forgiveness it will be granted, but you ask anyway. Your victim's process and path to forgiving may be operating on a different timeline than your own. If forgiveness is refused, do not press your victim or respond with anything other than humility and understanding. Let them know that you are there to assist them in whatever way needed, that you respect their decision, and then show by your actions that you have changed. It is never wise, nor is it helpful, to force the issue. You cannot force someone to forgive you. Often, and especially within intimate relationships, it takes time to rebuild trust. If you have betrayed someone close to you, it could take weeks, months, or even years before they consider granting forgiveness and renewing the relationship.

Even without someone granting you forgiveness, you can still move along the Fourfold Path. The fact that you will not be forgiven in the way you wish does not have to prevent your own growth and healing. None of us can continue to bear the burden of a wrong for which we are truly penitent and contrite. If you have honestly tried and failed in your request for forgiveness, then you have fulfilled your part. This does not mean there are not reparations to make. We must always try to give back what we have taken from someone else, whether it is tangible or intangible. We must always seek to make amends. Sometimes we cannot give back what was lost, as is the case with Angela's death, but there are always amends that can be made.

How Do I Make Amends?

A big part of asking for forgiveness is making amends, and what this consists of depends in part on what the victim needs from you in order to forgive. It can be a tangible return of what was lost, such as paying back money that was stolen or returning property that was taken. These are often the easiest and clearest amends to make. If your amends are of a financial nature and you are not able to fulfill them immediately, it is helpful to make a plan with your victim for regular repayments and then stick to that plan. Our words can express our remorse and desire to do right, but it is often our actions that most show our true intentions. If you make an agreement, stick to it, or you may find yourself traveling the Fourfold Path all over again.

The amends needed may be of a more symbolic nature. For example, if there has been abuse or infidelity, your spouse or partner may need you to agree to go to counseling. If I were telling my father what I needed from him to heal our relationship, I may tell him that I needed him never to drink again.

In general, a victim needs to know and be reassured that the offense won't happen again. What your victim needs will be unique to your situation. Often simply understanding the circumstances and the reasons for your actions, as well as feeling your genuine remorse, is all that is needed to grant forgiveness and move on to restoring the relationship.

The amends process cannot be skipped or glossed over. If you are engaging in the Fourfold Path without being able to directly ask for forgiveness or ask the one you have hurt what they need to be made whole, you can still make indirect amends to your victim, as we saw Lisa Cotter do with Mandie and Carrie, the two girls killed in the car accident for which she was responsible. If you have stolen money, you can donate an equivalent amount to a charity in the name of the person from whom you stole. You can send that amount anonymously to the victim or the victim's family. If you have caused harm in your community, you can volunteer to work in your community as a form of reparation. There are countless ways we can set matters right, even without direction from those we have harmed. Ultimately, you are engaging in this process to return to your wholeness and heal all who were harmed—including yourself. Making amends is also how you heal yourself.

Four: Renewing or Releasing the Relationship

The last step in the Fourfold Path is renewing or releasing the relationship. As we said in the previous chapter, and this is true whether you are a victim or a perpetrator, the preference is always for the renewal and restoration of a connection. Often our relationships can grow stronger through the process of admitting a wrong and asking for forgiveness. When we are forgiven, we can begin anew and learn from the mistakes of the past. It is important to note that renewing is not forgetting. When we are forgiven, we move forward into a new relationship, but we cannot expect the people we have hurt to forget that hurt. We do not ask our victims to forget but rather to recognize the humanity we share and our willingness to change. It is our hope that after an honest practice of the Fourfold process of forgiving, both parties will move forward and create a new story together. It is not always possible, but it is always worth striving toward.

We seek restoration and renewal, and if that is not possible, we release the relationship. Just as renewing the relationship is not forgetting, releasing the relationship is not losing. Sometimes we cannot create something new from the wreckage of the past, but we still must move forward into the possibilities of the future. None of us can force a relationship. If the person you have harmed chooses not to have a relationship with you, this is that person's choice. With grace and in full knowledge, you have done all you can to make it right. You must honor that person's decision to release you and the relationship.

Releasing means moving into a future free of the past. You have done all you could to heal the relationship. The Fourfold Path is your stepping-stone to a new life and a return to who you truly are. In the next chapter, we will explore how to walk the Fourfold Path to find the transformation that comes from forgiving yourself.

But first, let us pause and listen to what the heart hears.

I am sorry
How many deaths have those words died?
They were stuck in my throat
They melted on my tongue
They suffocated before they met the air
I am sorry
The words crouch on my heart
And they weigh a ton
Could I not just get on with it, say I'm sorry and be done?
I am sorry and I am not done
I am sorry for the hurt I caused
For the doubts I inspired, for the sadness you held
For the anger, despair, suffering, and grief you endured
I am sorry
There is no currency with which I can repay you for your tears
But I can make amends
And I do mean it when I say
I am sorry

Summary

Needing Forgiveness

- Gather support as needed.
- Admit the wrong.
- Witness the anguish and apologize.
- Ask for forgiveness.
- Make amends or whatever restitution or reparation is called for or needed.
- Honor your victim's choice to renew or release the relationship.

Meditation

The Box of Forgiveness

1. *Create a safe space.* Bring to mind a place of safety. (If you did this meditation in chapter 4, recall it now. If not, read on.) Your place of safety can be real or imaginary. See this place fully and inhabit it. Are you indoors or outdoors? Is it a large, open space or a cozy place? What does it smell like? What does the air feel like on your skin? What sounds do you hear? Music? A crackling fire? Birdsong? A babbling brook or a fountain? Ocean waves? The hushed whisper of grass swaying in a breeze? There is an inviting place to sit comfortably. Relax into this place. It is your place of safety.

2. *Someone is calling for you.* The one who is calling for you speaks in a voice filled with warmth, love, and delight. When you are ready, welcome this person into your safe place. Notice how the person's presence increases your sense of safety and assurance. Who is your companion? Is it a loved one, a friend, or a spiritual figure? It is someone who is accepting, affirming, and utterly trustworthy.

3. *Between you and your companion sits an open box.* Look at the box. It is small and light enough for you to lift and hold. Notice its size, shape, and texture. What is unique about this box? Tell your companion the story of what you have done. Tell the truth about the harm you have caused in as much detail as you can. As you

speak, see the guilt and shame pouring out of you like a stream. Watch the stream being poured into the open box. Speak until you have finished.

4. *Ask for forgiveness.* Tell your companion that you are sorry for what you have done and ask for forgiveness. Your companion smiles at you, knowing that you are whole and worthy of love no matter what you have done. Now gently close the box of forgiveness.

5. *Take the box into your lap.* You may want to sit with it in your lap for a few moments. When you are ready, hand the box to your trusted companion.

6. *When you are ready, you may leave your place of safety.* Know that your trusted companion will hold your box of forgiveness and welcomes you at the end of your Fourfold Path.

Stone Ritual

Setting Down the Stone

1. For this ritual you will need a heavy stone. You want to feel its weight as burdensome.
2. Walk with this stone some distance to a private place.
3. Admit to the stone what you have done.
4. Then tell the stone the anguish you have caused.
5. Then apologize to the stone and ask for forgiveness. You can imagine the person you have harmed in your mind's eye, or ask God for forgiveness.
6. Decide what you can do to make amends to the person you harmed or how you can help others.
7. Then set the stone down in nature.

Journal Exercise

Meditations and visualizations can be healing, but it is also extremely helpful to write down what you have done as a preparation for apologizing and asking for forgiveness.

1. *Admitting the wrong.* What have you done? Use this place in your journal to tell the truth and list the facts of the harm you have caused.

2. *Witnessing the anguish.* Now look deeply at how your actions have harmed the other. Write sentences that begin "I am sorry for . . ." Write as many sentences as you can.

3. *Asking for forgiveness.* Write the following sentence and finish it: "I would understand if you are not able to forgive me now, but I hope you will be able to forgive me someday because . . ."

4. *Renewing or releasing the relationship.* You will be asking the person what you can do to make it right, but here you will list your own ideas for how you can renew the relationship. What could you do to repair what you have broken?

Chapter 9

Forgiving Yourself

MY FATHER SAID he wanted to talk. I was exhausted. We were halfway home on that pilgrimage we made six times each year. We had driven ten hours that day to drop the children at their boarding school in Swaziland. Sleep beckoned. We would rest for a few hours before continuing the next day for another fifteen-hour drive back to our home in Alice. It was a year after the incident with the white boy in the market. Another drive through the Karoo was still ahead of us and the journey was always trying.

I told my father I was tired and had a headache. "We'll talk tomorrow, in the morning," I said. We headed to Leah's mother's home a half hour away. The next morning my niece came to wake us with the news: my father was dead.

I was grief-stricken. I loved my father very much, and while his temper pained me greatly, there was so much about him that was loving, wise, and witty. And then there was the guilt. With his sudden death I would never be able to hear what he had wanted to say. Was there some great stone on his heart that he had wanted to remove? Might he have wanted to apologize for the abuse he had inflicted on my mother when I was a boy? I will never know. It has taken me many, many years to forgive myself for my insensitivity, for not honoring my father one last time with the few moments he wanted to share with me. Honestly, the guilt still stings.

When I reflect back across the years to his drunken tirades, I realize now that it was not just with him that I was angry. I was angry with myself. Cowering in fear as a boy, I had not been able to stand up to my father or protect my mother. So many years later, I realize that I not only have to forgive my father. I have to forgive myself.

We are called to forgive each other time and time again; it is the nature of being in a relationship. Yes, it can be very hard to forgive others, but often it can be harder still to forgive ourselves. If I eat too many sweets, do I berate myself for a lack of willpower or offer myself forgiveness for giving in to the demands of my sweet tooth? If I say, "Today I will go to the gym and get fit" but instead take a nice long nap, do I need to punish or forgive myself? If I forgive myself, does that mean I will take an even longer nap tomorrow after eating even more sweets?

The reasons for forgiving ourselves are the same as for forgiving others. It is how we become free of the past. It is how we heal and grow. It is how we make meaning out of our suffering, restore our self-esteem, and tell a new story of who we are. If forgiving others leads to an external peace, forgiving ourselves leads to an internal peace. It can be so very difficult when you are both the victim and the perpetrator in your own story.

Something Was Wrong with Me

Almost immediately, Margaret Healy's family forgave seventeen-year-old Kelly Connor for the road accident that killed Margaret. Decades later, Kelly still struggles with forgiving herself:

> I felt like I didn't deserve to be happy or to even have a life. It was a painful way of living in the world. I felt separate from everyone and everything. A big part of it was not being able to talk about it, but the other part was that I was so very ashamed. Something was wrong with me. Was I truly this horrid monster who had killed another person? I wasn't completely truthful about the accident, and I know that contributed to my self-loathing and my guilt and shame.
>
> My entire life was defined by that one afternoon. I don't know who I would be if it hadn't happened. It's taken me decades to become okay with who I am. Does this mean I've forgiven myself? I'm not sure. It is something I still struggle with to this day. I know I wouldn't be who I am without having taken a life, and today I like who I am. It's hard to reconcile. When I speak about the accident, it helps others, and this helps tremendously in my self-forgiveness.
>
> Today there is new research into the unique trauma that occurs when drivers cause accidental deaths. This research is happening because I shared my experience publicly. Knowing some good can come out of this tragedy gives me

something to hold on to—a larger meaning and purpose. I know Margaret's family forgave me. I believe Margaret herself forgives me. And most days I believe I have forgiven me. It's been a long, hard process, though. If this had happened to a friend, I would have told them, "Accidents happen. Forgive yourself. Move on." I guess we are hardest on ourselves. I know I am. I try to help others. I'm a good mother. These are the things I remind myself of when the self-recrimination starts up in my mind, and it does help.

Self-Forgiveness Is Not a Free Pass

When we forgive someone, we let go of any demand that he or she should suffer as we have suffered. As we have shown, this cycle of retribution and revenge never offers the release from pain we seek. It only serves to compound the anguish. When we forgive ourselves, we also free ourselves from a cycle of punishment and retribution directed at ourselves. This is not to say we are not responsible and accountable for our actions. If I come into your house and steal your belongings, I cannot then go home and say, "Well, I forgive myself, so all is right in the world."

Forgiving myself does not let me off the hook for what I've done. I still must walk the Fourfold Path and seek to right my wrongs with my victim. If you have not done this, please return to the previous chapter and venture on the path to seeking forgiveness. To truly forgive ourselves, we cannot skip over an honest attempt to admit our wrongs, confront the consequences of our hurtful actions, apologize, ask for forgiveness, and make amends.

Professors Julie Hall and Frank Fincham from the

State University of New York at Buffalo are studying self-forgiveness, what they call the "stepchild" of forgiveness research. In their published study, they distinguish between true self-forgiveness and pseudo self-forgiveness:

> In order to truly forgive oneself, one must either explicitly or implicitly acknowledge that one's behavior was wrong and accept responsibility or blame for such behavior. Without these elements, self-forgiveness is irrelevant and pseudo self-forgiveness becomes likely. Pseudo self-forgiveness occurs when an offender fails to acknowledge wrongdoing and accept responsibility. In such a situation, one may indicate that one has forgiven oneself when, in fact, one does not believe one did anything wrong. The realization of wrongdoing and acceptance of responsibility generally initiate feelings of guilt and regret, which must be fully experienced before one can move toward self-forgiveness. Attempts to forgive oneself without cognitively and emotionally processing the transgression and its consequences are likely to lead to denial, suppression, or pseudo self-forgiveness.[12]

We are looking for authentic self-forgiveness, and this comes only with an honest, searching look at ourselves, our actions, and the consequences of our actions. People who genuinely seek to forgive themselves are people who want to change. They don't want to repeat the mistakes of the past. To want genuine self-forgiveness you must be a person of conscience. If you feel guilt, shame, regret, or remorse for something you have done, this is the place to begin. You can walk the Fourfold Path and seek forgiveness. If you are paralyzed by guilt, shame, regret, or remorse, there is a way to heal and break free of the paralysis by engaging in a process of forgiving yourself.

Why Should I Forgive Myself
and Why Is It So Difficult?

Lack of self-forgiveness can affect every area of our lives—
our health, careers, relationships, parenting, and our general
happiness and well-being. When we are unforgiving of ourselves, we experience the same harmful emotional and physical effects as when we are unforgiving of others. Holding on
to self-blame keeps us stuck in a prison of the past and limits
the potential that lies within the present moment. We can
so easily make ourselves victims of our own thoughts and
feelings of guilt and shame for what we have done. Make no
mistake, we must be accountable for our actions, but when
we stay stuck in the unhappy story of what we have done—
when we make an identity out of our past actions—we deny
ourselves the gift of transformation. We can all learn from
the mistakes of our past. Learning from the past is not the
same as being held hostage by what we have done. At some
stage we must let go of the past and begin again. We have
said repeatedly that no one is undeserving of forgiveness, and
this includes you.

I know it can still be difficult to offer ourselves the forgiveness we can so freely give to others. Perhaps we hold
ourselves to a higher standard than the standard to which we
hold other people. (If we think carefully, we recognize this
double standard as a small piece of arrogance: I am a better
person than he or she is, so I should behave better.) Perhaps we feel we have not truly paid for our crimes. Perhaps
our guilt and shame are keeping us from feeling we deserve
another chance. Brené Brown, a leading shame researcher
and the author of many wonderful books on the subject,

defines guilt as the feeling that "I've done something bad" and shame as the feeling that "I am bad."

It is appropriate and inevitable to feel guilty when we do wrong. It is how we know we need to walk the Fourfold Path to repair the harm we have caused and renew our relationships. Guilt helps us stay connected with others. Shame also plays its evolutionary role in keeping us in relationship to the group. "Have you no shame" is what we say to people who have no sense of how their actions harm others. But shame can be toxic. Toxic shame drives us out of connection and community and makes us believe we do not belong. It makes us think we do not deserve to be in relationships.

No one is bad, and none among us should be defined as the sum total of our worst actions. Kelly Connor is not a killer; she is a person whose actions killed another person. None of us is an offender, liar, betrayer, or monster. We are all fragile and flawed humans who may lie or steal or betray. We are fragile and flawed humans who commit offenses against others. When we do these things, we are not monsters; we are human beings who have become separated from our own goodness.

We are not defined by what we have done. We have all been so conditioned to believe that we are held in high esteem because of the things we do, not because of who we are. In truth, our worth has nothing to do with performance, but this belief can make it very difficult to forgive ourselves when we do wrong. None of us is constantly our best self. None of us is perfect. Sometimes the failures for which we must forgive ourselves are not willful failures. We did the best we knew to do at the time. The night that fatigue made me turn away from my father, I was doing the best I knew to do. I was in no fit state for a meaningful conversation. I did not know that there would be no other opportunity. I have come to accept this. We all have to accept the past in order to create a new future. If we could have done things better, we would have. Even if we have inflicted harm deliberately, we all have the potential to change. We can work to right our wrongs or make amends. None of us is perfect, but we can perfect the art of learning from our past mistakes, and we can perfect the art of self-forgiveness. This is how we grow and change and, ultimately, begin anew.

Can You Look in the Mirror?

It took Lisa Cotter five years in prison before she could meet her own eyes in the mirror. Dan and Lynn Wagner, the parents of the two girls Lisa killed in a car accident, offered their forgiveness to Lisa through a letter sent to her in prison, but the path to self-forgiveness was not traveled as swiftly. Lisa explains:

> If I could stop time, I would go back to that night and not drink and drive. But I can't. I have to live with the guilt and the shame. Every day, in so many ways, I have to own what I've done, and I have to find a way to move through the painful feelings that still come up or else I couldn't be a mother to my own children. And I feel guilty saying that. Because of me, Lynn and Dan can't be parents to their children, so how do I have a right to talk about my own struggles in parenting?
>
> In prison, the only way to live with my guilt was to have structure. I ran miles and miles every day around the

track in the prison yard. Every mile I cried and cried. I cried for the two girls who I killed. I cried for Dan and Lynn's suffering. I cried for my teenage son and my two little babies, who not only lost their mother, but whose mother had become this horrible monster and killer in the eyes of our community. I ran marathons of pure tears and grief.

I also read spiritual books and twelve-step workbooks, and in one workbook on healing and forgiving yourself, it said to look at yourself in the mirror and say, "I love you." Every morning during my daily routine, I would stand in front of the small sink in my cell that I shared with five other women and say, "I love you, Lisa." A cell-mate of mine had been watching me do this every day, week after week, year after year, and one day she started clapping and said, "You finally mean it." I didn't even realize that for five years I hadn't been able to look myself in the eye as I said the words—until that morning. "Now the real work begins," she said. I had no idea how true that was.

When I was released and met Dan and Lynn in the parole office, they hugged me and we all cried together. My self-forgiveness was definitely made easier by their forgiveness. We began a new relationship that day, and Lynn has become a spiritual mother of sorts to me. She's involved in my children's lives. She and Dan even wanted to meet my fiancé, to be sure he was a good guy. Together we share our story and we try to help others. I try to be of service to my community every time I'm asked, and I am completely honest about my past. I own it and I hold my head up when people talk about me behind my back or judge me. I understand where they're coming from. It helps that, to Dan and Lisa, I know I'm not "that woman" or "that terrorist" any longer. I'm just Lisa, and I have my story and they have their story, and together we have our story.

What Self-Forgiveness Is and Is Not

Forgiving yourself is not a way to excuse what you have done or gloss over the harm you have caused others. It is not forgetting about your actions. In fact, it is an honest remembering of what you have done and how you have hurt others. Self-forgiveness is not a loophole to avoid admitting wrongs or making restitution. Self-forgiveness is true self-acceptance. What that means is that you come to accept yourself as a flawed human being. Lisa came to a place of self-acceptance when she could look at herself in the mirror and say, "I love you." In that hopeful moment, healing and transformation became possible. If you are suffering because of the harm you have caused another, that means you have remorse and a conscience, and within those painful feelings is the healing balm you are looking for.

Hatred is poison. If you direct hatred at yourself, then self-forgiveness is the antidote to that toxin.

What Does Self-Forgiveness Require?

First and foremost, self-forgiveness requires absolute truth. We need truth before we can reconcile with others, and we need truth before we can reconcile with ourselves. If you haven't admitted your wrongs and asked for forgiveness, then do so now. However, whether you've been granted for-

giveness by another or not, you can still endeavor to forgive yourself. The forgiveness of others is not a requirement
for self-forgiveness. It can make self-forgiveness easier, of
course, but some people may never forgive you. As we've
said throughout the book, we forgive for ourselves, not for
others. We cannot force someone to forgive us; that person's forgiveness is his or her journey. We cannot force self-
forgiveness. We can walk the path that allows self-forgiveness
to unfold.

Self-forgiveness requires that we face the truth of how we
are feeling. Do we feel guilt? Do we feel shame? Do we feel
grief? Do we feel despair or hopelessness? When we identify
the feelings hindering our self-forgiveness, we can begin to
work with them and transform them. Our feelings of guilt or
shame may never go away completely, and we must be careful not to compound matters by feeling guilt or shame about
still feeling guilt or shame.

Self-forgiveness also requires humility and hard work. It
requires a sincere desire not to repeat the behavior and a sincere desire to change. If I lied to my spouse, in order to truly
forgive myself I must look at the pain I caused her. I must
be honest about the damage I've caused to our relationship
and resolve not to lie to her again. When we know we are
doing all we can to make our amends, we make it possible to
forgive ourselves for our actions.

Self-forgiveness also requires stepping into unknown ter-
ritory. We can make an identity out of being "bad." We
can reduce our self-description to consist of only our worst
actions. When we forgive ourselves, we let go of that identity. It can be frightening to discover the vast beauty of who

we really are. There can be a strange comfort within the discomfort of perpetual self-blame and self-punishment. Any profound change can be disconcerting.

How Do I Forgive Myself?

When we recognize we are suffering because of our lack of self-forgiveness, we have taken the first step along the path of forgiving ourselves. We must then choose to do the work required in self-forgiving. Identifying our feelings and embracing them will help us choose the way to either live with or transform them.

Guilt

We all feel guilty at times. I feel guilty if I get angry with my colleague or if I yell at the children or if I am rude to a stranger on the street. Guilt is a word associated with *doing*—we feel guilty when we *do* something wrong or when we hurt someone we care about. Brené Brown writes, "Guilt is good. Guilt helps us stay on track, because it's about our behavior. It occurs when we compare something we've done—or failed to do—with our personal values. The discomfort that results often motivates real change, amends, and self-reflection."[13] Guilt is derived from the German word *gelt,* which means recompense or a repayment of a debt. If we are unable to forgive ourselves because we feel guilt, then the solution is to look at whom we need to recompense for our actions. Do we need to apologize? Pay someone back the money we stole? Do we need to own up to our actions directly to the person we harmed and witness the anguish

Resolving Guilt

Ask yourself what you have done or not done that is making you feel guilty, and then ask yourself what actions you can take to make it right. If you are unsure what to do, ask a friend or a trusted advisor for advice. Finally, take the action you have resolved to take—and remember, the solution for guilt is always found in *doing*, in making amends.

we've caused? Since feelings of guilt come from specific things we have done or not done, they can only be resolved by taking action. In short, more doing.

Shame

Shame is a bit trickier to identify than guilt. Unlike guilt, shame is a feeling associated with *being* rather than doing. When I feel ashamed, it means I feel there isn't just something wrong with what I've done, there is something wrong with who I am. Shame is often a hidden emotion and it can be paralyzing in its power. When we feel a profound sense of shame, we feel a profound disconnection from ourselves and the world. We feel, at our core, that we are not worthy of forgiveness from others or from ourselves.

The biggest barrier to self-forgiveness can be these feelings of shame. Shame makes us small and makes us want to hide, because we believe we are not worthy of belonging in the community or the world. Unexpressed shame can lead to isolation, depression, substance abuse, or suicide. Unexpressed or unidentified shame can make it impossible for us to feel we are worthy of self-forgiveness. We lessen the power shame has on us when we give it a voice. Shame hides while truth does not.

The process of self-forgiveness and lessening shame involves reaching out to a group of like-minded or accepting people and sharing your identity and experiences. When you connect with others who also struggle with forgiving themselves because they are ashamed of who they are and what they've done, that connection can transform the shame. This is why twelve-step groups are so successful the world over—people are able to come together and identify with each other in a place where they feel they belong, regardless of who they are or what they've done. When you share your experiences with others, you create new meaning out of a painful past. When Lisa Cotter stands before an audience and says she killed two teenage girls, her shame is lessened because she is finding a place where she belongs and is helping others not to make the same mistakes she did. This, in turn, gives her a new sense of value and purpose in the world. We feel shame

Resolving Shame

Share your feelings with others. Be of service and help others, and this will strengthen your sense of self-worth and value. Remember, you can heal shame only in connection with others, and when you connect with others, your compassion for others and for yourself increases. When you feel compassion for yourself, you are more easily forgiving of yourself and your past behavior.

in isolation. It can only be healed in a community and in connection with others. Because we feel shame, we can be compassionate with the shame felt by others. Because we feel compassionate toward others, we then can feel compassion for ourselves. When we feel self-compassion, we then can experience forgiveness for ourselves.

We all want to live in peace and harmony. But living in peace with others requires having peace and harmony within ourselves. We can transform our guilt and our shame by using our past to be of benefit to others. When we place ourselves and our stories in the service of others, we can more easily forgive ourselves for our failings. One of the people who killed Amy Biehl, Ntobeko Peni, has found a way to reconcile both his past and his future through a new mission and purpose:

> I felt I had contributed to a new South Africa and that what I did was done for a political reason. But when I thought of Amy . . . I realized one has to find peace within in order to live. It's odd, but sometimes people who offer forgiveness are so disappointed when the people they forgive cannot forgive themselves. This foundation helped me forgive myself.

Ntobeko Peni is speaking of his work with the Amy Biehl Foundation. By working for the foundation named for the girl he killed, he has been able to transform his guilt and shame. He has been able to face his past actions honestly and forgive himself. He was forgiven by Amy's family—as Kelly Connor was forgiven by Margaret's family and Lisa Cotter was forgiven by the Wagners. All of them had to put themselves and their stories into the service of their communities in order to forgive themselves. By speaking their shame, they have been able to create new stories of themselves. They are no longer completely defined by their worst deeds. They have stepped into the frightening potential of being their best selves.

Each of us can find a way to transform a painful past into a hopeful future. We can develop compassion for others and compassion for ourselves. We can tell a new story of ourselves. The new story admits that "yes, I have caused pain and suffering." The new story also recognizes that "the harm I have caused in the past is not who I am today." Self-forgiveness is truly at the core of peacemaking, and we cannot build peace with others if we are not at peace with ourselves. In the next chapter, we will see how we can create a world of peace by making a world of forgiveness.

But first, let us pause to listen to what the heart hears.

I am generous to you
And miserly to me
I can banish the harm you caused me
from the smallest corners of my heart
It has no root or residence in me
But the deed I have done
Fills me with shame and pain
I cannot make myself whole again
I cannot forgive myself
If my tender heart is truly there for you
It must be tender for me too
Soft and yielding
Kind and forgiving
I must allow myself to come face-to-face
with my own humanity
I can break free

Summary

Forgiving Yourself

- We become imprisoned in the past when we do not forgive ourselves for past mistakes.
- If you have not sought forgiveness from your victim, do so. Forgiving yourself will be easier after you have sought forgiveness from your victim.
- We do not heal in isolation. Connecting with others is how we develop compassion for others and for ourselves.

Meditation

Breathing Compassion

1. For this meditation you will need to get still and centered.
2. Find a quiet place to sit or lie comfortably.
3. Follow your breath.
4. As you breathe in, visualize love and compassion entering you like a golden light.
5. With each inhalation, you will see the golden light begin to fill you from your toes to the top of your head.
6. When you are filled, you radiate this love and compassion outward effortlessly.

Stone Ritual

The Hand of Mercy

1. Find a small stone that fits in the palm of your hand.
2. Hold it in your left hand. This is the hand of judgment.
3. For each item on your list of things you need to forgive yourself for, transfer the stone from your left hand to your right hand.
4. The right hand is the hand of mercy and forgiveness.
5. Holding the stone in your right hand, say the words "I forgive myself for . . ." and fill in an item from your list.
6. When you are done, return the stone to where you found it.

Journal Exercise

1. Make a list of all the things for which you need to forgive yourself.

2. For each thing you have listed, decide whether the forgiveness you need is from someone else or yourself. If it is from someone else, then walk the Fourfold Path. If it is truly from yourself, then it is time to rediscover your goodness.

3. Write a list of all that is good about you. Look at yourself through the eyes of a loving and admiring companion.

Chapter 10

A World of Forgiveness

I BROKE DOWN. I was the president of the All Africa Conference of Churches and I was making a pastoral visit to Rwanda in 1995, just one year after the genocide. I went to Ntarama, a town where hundreds of Tutsis had fled to the church for safety and sanctuary. But the Hutu Power movement had respected no church. Strewn across the floor were the remains of the horror. Clothing and suitcases were still littered among the bones. The small skulls of children remained shattered on the floor. Skulls outside the church still had machetes and knives in them. The stench was beyond anything I can describe. I tried to pray, but I could not. I could only cry.

Rwanda, like the Holocaust and other genocides before it, stands as a testament to our capacity for unconscionable evil, and yet our ability to forgive and heal stands as a rejoinder that we are not made for evil but for goodness. These spasms of cruelty and violence, hatred and ruthlessness, are the exception not the rule of our human lives. Indeed, the Gacaca traditional community courts established in Rwanda are an extraordinary example of the ability of a nation that was once convulsed in genocidal violence to heal itself through reconciliation and forgiveness. More than twelve thousand community-based courts tried over 1.2 million cases throughout the country. The justice they sought was often restorative rather than punitive. Those who had planned and incited the genocide were punished, but those who were swept up in the internecine conflict were given lower sentences, especially if the perpetrators were repentant and sought reconciliation with the community. The goal was to rebuild the communities and the country, to heal and prevent further revenge and violence. This is an example of how forgiveness can help heal an entire country.

Forgiveness is at the core of peacemaking. I have seen this in my own country, in Rwanda, in Northern Ireland, and in the hearts of so many who travel the long and difficult road to find the peace that comes through forgiving.

Take Care of Each Other

We must all be careful with our words. Hurtful words may not be forgotten, but they can be forgiven. I still remember the words of the boy in the market in the Karoo, but I have forgiven him. We must all strive to be careful with our actions. When we assault another's humanity, we assault our own humanity. Every person wants to be acknowledged and affirmed for who and what they are, a human being of infinite worth, someone with a place in the world. We can't violate another's dignity without violating our own. Violence, whether in words or deeds, only begets more violence. Violence can never engender peace. Still, I will always pray for the person who holds the weapon, pray that this person finds compassion and recognizes the humanity he or she shares with the person who may be at the other end of that weapon's sights. Henry Wadsworth Longfellow said, "If we could read the secret history of our enemies, we should find in each man's life sorrow and suffering enough to disarm all hostility."

When we have hatred for others, we carry that hatred in our own hearts and it harms us even more, certainly, than it does them. We are created for fellowship. We are created to form the human family, existing together because we were made for one another. We are not made for exclusivity or self-sufficiency but for interdependence. We break this essential law of our being at our own peril. We take care of our world by taking care of each other—it is as simple and as difficult as that.

Cultivating Forgiveness

How we take care of each other is by cultivating our forgiveness. Forgiveness, like any other quality—compassion, kindness, or generosity—must be fostered and developed. The ability to forgive is innate but, like any natural talent, it is perfected with practice. The practice of forgiveness is emotional and spiritual work. When Nelson Mandela went to jail, he was a very angry man. This global role model of forgiveness was not very forgiving on the day he stepped onto Robben Island to begin his prison sentence. It took the many years in jail, years he spent cultivating a daily practice of forgiveness, for him to become the luminous example of tolerance who was able to put our wounded country on the road to reconciliation and healing. The man who walked into prison was not the man who invited his prison guard to be a VIP guest at his inauguration. That took time and effort.

Each one of us has multiple opportunities each day to practice small acts of forgiveness. We can learn to move through the Forgiveness Cycle with an emotional sure-footedness born of practice. I can forgive the driver who cut me off in morning traffic. I acknowledge the spark of irritation and fear evoked in me, even while I recognize that I don't know her story. She may have been late to work for a tyrannical boss. She may have been distracted by her baby wailing in the backseat. She may have a list of things to do today that is longer than her arm. To practice cultivating forgiveness, I must learn to look at the bigger picture and know that not every action that bothers me is a personal attack. I can practice forgiveness with my friends and family, and I can practice it in my workplace and community.

When I develop a mind-set of forgiveness, rather than a mind-set of grievance, I don't just forgive a particular act; I become a more forgiving person. With a grievance mind-set, I look at the world and see all that is wrong. When I have a forgiveness mind-set, I start to see the world not through grievance but through gratitude. In other words, I look at the world and start to see what is right. There is a special kind of magic that happens when I become a more forgiving person—it is something quite remarkable. What was once a grave affront melts into nothing more than a thoughtless or careless act. What was once a reason for rupture and alienation becomes an opportunity for repair and greater intimacy. A life that seemed littered with obstacles and antagonism is suddenly filled with opportunity and love.

When I cultivate forgiveness in my small everyday encounters, I am preparing for the time when a much larger act of forgiveness will be asked of me, as it almost certainly will. It seems none of us journeys through life unscathed by tragedy, disappointment, betrayal, or heartbreak, but each of us has at his or her disposal a most powerful skill that lessens and can even transmute the pain. This skill can, when given the chance, win over an enemy, heal a marriage, stop a fight, and—on a global scale—even end a war. When you set out to change the world, the job seems insurmountable. But each of us can do his or her small part to effect change. We change the world when we choose to create a world of forgiveness in our own hearts and minds. It is our nature to forgive, reconcile, and rebuild the broken pieces of our relationships. Every hand that extends itself in a gesture of forgiveness is a hand working toward the creation of peace in the world.

Transforming Suffering

Even when we thoroughly forgive, our grief may not end, our loss may still be unacceptable, and the hurt may still be there. But we discover time and again amazing accounts of people who have found a way to make meaning out of their suffering and transform it. Elizabeth Kübler-Ross sums it up beautifully when she says, "The most beautiful people we have known are those who have known defeat, known suffering, known struggle, known loss, and have found their way out of the depths. These persons have an appreciation, a sensitivity, and an understanding of life that fills them with compassion, gentleness, and a deep loving concern. Beautiful people do not just happen."[14]

Some of the people whose stories we've shared in this book are examples of those who have gained a profound ability to walk the Fourfold Path of forgiving, to transform their losses, and transmute their pain.

Kia Scherr made something meaningful out of her loss. After the deaths of her husband and daughter in a terrorist attack in Mumbai, Kia established an organization with a profound message of peace:

> If we continue to love in the face of terrorism, we disempower the terrorist and the terrorist ceases to terrorize. Imagine multiplying this a million-billionfold around the world and, over time, we will truly end terrorism. Onelife alliance.org is using the power of connection to unite people of all ages, from all countries, backgrounds, nationalities, and religions, to respect the dignity and sanctity of life and to create a world of harmonious balance and cooperation. Now is the time to counter terrorism in all forms by choosing to live with peace, compassion, and love. This is my work after Alan and Naomi's deaths. This is my purpose.

Bassam Aramin, who cofounded Combatants for Peace, has used his own powerful story of recognizing the humanity of his enemies to create an organization devoted to dialogue, reconciliation, and nonviolence. This organization is run by former Israeli soldiers and Palestinian fighters who say, "After brandishing weapons for so many years, and having seen one another only through weapon sights, we have decided to put down our guns and to fight for peace."[15]

All the stories shared in this book are profound examples of walking the Fourfold Path. You don't need to start a foundation or travel to distant lands. Transformation begins in you, wherever you are, whatever has happened, however you are suffering. Transformation is always possible. We do not heal in isolation. When we reach out and connect with one another—when we tell the story, name the hurt, grant forgiveness, and renew or release the relationship—our suffering begins to transform. We don't have to carry our pain alone. We don't have to bind ourselves to our losses forever. Our freedom is forged in the fires of forgiving, and we grow into more spiritually evolved people because of it. When our losses are great, the depth of our compassion for others can increase exponentially, as can our ability to use our own suffering to transform the suffering of other people. It is true that when we harm others, we harm ourselves; but it is just as true that when we help others, we also help ourselves.

How We Create a World of Forgiveness

Creating a world of forgiveness does not require spending one's life in contemplation of the values and virtues of forgiving. Creating a world of forgiveness is a living practice. You can create a world of forgiveness in your own home today. Forgive your child who comes home late or yells at you once again. Forgive your spouse for the hurtful words they speak.

Forgive your neighbor for keeping you up late at night with a noisy party when you have to work in the morning. Forgive the stranger who robs your home. Forgive the boyfriend who leaves you. Know that we are all flawed and we are all just struggling to find our place in the sun—a place where we can be acknowledged and affirmed for who and what we are.

Cultivate your forgiveness with your friends, with your family, with strangers, and with yourself. Remind yourself that every person you encounter carries a sorrow and a struggle. Recognize that we all share a fundamental humanity. Model the Fourfold Path with your children. Show them the healing that comes from letting go of thoughts of revenge, releasing grudges, and reconciling relationships that have been damaged or broken. If you hurt someone, show your children how to admit the wrong, ask for forgiveness, and make amends.

Let us teach children the process of forgiveness. Let us guide them away from the Revenge Cycle and reward them when they enter the Forgiveness Cycle.

Restoring Our World

Nationally and globally we have a choice: restorative or retributive justice.

There are those who believe an injustice can be made right only when someone is made to pay for the harm that person has caused. They say I will forgive you provided you get clobbered for what you have done, provided you are made to pay and pay dearly for the harm you have caused me. This is not the path to creating a world of forgiveness or the path to real justice.

This eye-for-an-eye system is the basis of retributive justice. In many countries, and especially in the West, the criminal justice system controls crime and punishment. Offenders are accountable only to the State. Those found guilty take their just punishment as decided by the State and according to the laws set forth in advance by the State. When a law is broken, it is a crime against the State. Crime is seen as an individual act with consequences for the individual criminal. Punishment is meted out and the offender is defined by his or her guilt. In this system of justice, punishment is believed to be both a deterrent to crime and a way of changing future behavior. Sadly, overcrowded prisons and high rates of recidivism tell a different story.

Restorative justice, on the other hand, begins from the premise that a crime is an act not against the State but against another person and against the community. In this model of justice, accountability is based on the offender taking responsibility both for the harm they have caused and for taking action to repair the hurt. Victims are not peripheral to this process of justice. In the restorative justice model, victims play an integral role in deciding what is needed to repair the harm done to them. The focus is on dialogue, problem-solving, reconciling relationships, making restitution, and repairing the fabric of the community. Restorative justice seeks to recognize the humanity in each of us, whether we are victims or perpetrators. Restorative justice strives to bring about real healing and true justice to individuals and communities.

Forgiveness does not usually play a part in retributive justice, but it is central to restorative justice. Forgiveness in this context says, "I am giving you a second chance. I hope you will use it to become your best self. If I do not introduce forgiveness into the pattern of harm you have created, the cycle of retribution can go on ad infinitum." Without forgiveness to break the cycle of injury and vengeance, we set the scene for family feuds that last for generations. Without forgiveness, we create patterns of violence and hurt that get repeated in neighborhoods and cities and between countries for decades and even centuries.

It All Matters

If you are standing before me, beaten and bleeding, I cannot tell you to forgive. I cannot tell you to do anything, since you are the one who was beaten. If you have lost a loved one, I cannot tell you to forgive. You are the person who has lost a loved one. If your spouse betrayed you, if you were abused as a child, if you have endured any of the myriad injuries humans can inflict upon one another, I cannot tell you what to do. But I can tell you that it all matters. Whether we love or we hate, whether we help or we harm, it all matters. I can tell you that I hope, if I am the one who is beaten and bloodied, I will be able to forgive and pray for my abuser. I hope that I would be able to recognize him as my brother and as a precious child of God. I hope I never give up on the reality that every person has the capacity to change.

We can't create a world without pain or loss or conflict or hurt feelings, but we can create a world of forgiveness. We can create a world of forgiveness that allows us to heal from those losses and pain and repair our relationships. *The Book of Forgiving* shares the path to finding forgiveness, but ultimately no one can tell you to forgive. We can ask you to do so. We can invite you on the journey. We can show you what has worked for others. We can tell you that the healing we have seen from those who have walked the Fourfold Path is humbling and transformative.

All of us must walk our own paths, at our own pace. All of us write our own books of forgiving every single day. What will be in your book? Will it be a story of hope and redemption, or misery and resentment? In the end, the forgiveness you seek, whether it's for another or for yourself, will never be found in a book. You carry it with you in your heart. It is described by your humanity. You just need to look inside and discover it—discover the power it has to change your life and to change our world.

Let us listen to what the heart hears:

Here is my book of forgiving
The pages are well worn
Here are the places I struggled
Here are the places I passed through with ease
Here is my book of forgiving
Some of its pages are tear-stained and torn
Some are decorated with joy and laughter
Some of its pages are written with hope
Some are etched with despair
This is my book of forgiving
This book is full of stories and secrets
It tells how I finally broke free from being defined by injury
And chose to become a creator again
Offering forgiveness
Accepting that I am forgiven
Creating a world of peace

Resources

For more information on the authors and their work, please visit The Desmond and Leah Tutu Legacy Foundation (www.tutu.org.za).

For more resources on forgiveness, including interviews with the authors and a course on forgiveness with Mpho Tutu, please visit www.humanjourney.com/forgiveness.

Acknowledgments

IT WOULD BE IMPOSSIBLE to write a book on a subject as broad, as profound, and as intimate as forgiveness without the help of many people.

A global group of experts provided us with their hard-won knowledge, born from their pioneering work studying and teaching about forgiveness. We would like to thank all of those who contributed to the creation of this book including:

Fred Luskin for being generous with his time and for his profound insights. Donna Hicks for her ceaseless efforts to show people what it truly means to honor the dignity of another. Gordon Wheeler, one of the world's leading experts on shame, for his contribution to the chapter on self-forgiveness. Marina Cantacuzino, founder of The Forgiveness Project, for her gathering and sharing stories of forgiveness from around the world. Dr. Jim Dincalci who has spent over twenty-five years counseling and teaching people who are struggling to forgive. Brené Brown for her brave research into the heart of vulnerability and shame. Shawne Duperon for her passionate work creating Project Forgive and her creativity in using the media to spread the power of forgiveness around the world. Father Michael Lapsley for being a beautiful example of forgiveness and for creating out of his own suffering a ministry of healing. We also thank the Templeton Foundation for their generous grants to those studying the nature and science of forgiving.

It takes a special kind of courage and honesty to share personal grief, loss, and suffering so publicly. Our deepest gratitude to Lynn Wagner, Dan Wagner, Lisa Cotter, Ben Bosinger, Kia Scherr, Kelly Connor, Bassam Aramin, Easy Nofemla, Ntobeko Peni, and Linda Biehl. Your stories of forgiveness will help countless people to follow your example and transmute their pain into love and redemption.

Thank you to our extraordinary publishing team at HarperOne—Mark Tauber, Michael Maudlin, Claudia Boutote, Suzanne Wickham, Suzanne Quist, Julie Baker, Michele Wetherbee—it has been a joy and a privilege to work with you. We know that this book has been a personal quest for many of you, and we thank you for your support and belief in this project. Lynn Franklin, our agent extraordinaire, is what everyone would hope that their agent would be—an ally in the bewildering world of books. Lynn has been an expert guide, a cherished friend, and has become a member of our family.

There are two other people without whom this book would not have been possible. Lara Love was our researcher, our literary companion, and our supporter through many drafts. She is an aptly named genius with a heart of gold. She is really very, very gifted. We can credit Doug Abrams with holding the vision of this book through many years of gestation. He is a gifted editor and our talented literary collaborator. But more than that, Doug is a friend. The Fourfold Path begins with telling the story, and with his compassionate listening Doug has helped Mpho to walk a healing journey after Angela's death.

Finally, we want to thank the people with whom we trade daily lessons in forgiveness, the people who share our homes and fill them with love: Leah, Nyaniso, Onalenna, and Keke. Thank you for all you are and all you give.

Notes

1. http://www.forgiving.org/campaign/research.asp.
2. Frederic Luskin, *Forgive for Good: A Proven Prescription for Health and Happiness* (New York: HarperCollins, 2002).
3. Everett L. Worthington, Charlotte Van Oyen Witvliet, Pietro Pietrini, and Andrea J. Miller, "Forgiveness, Health, and Well-Being: A Review of Evidence for Emotional Versus Decisional Forgiveness, Dispositional Forgivingness, and Reduced Unforgiveness," *Journal of Behavioral Medicine* 30, no. 4 (August 2007): 291–302.
4. Lisa F. Berkman and Lester Breslow, *Health and Ways of Living: The Alameda County Study* (New York: Oxford Univ. Press, 1983).
5. Greg Miller, "Why Loneliness Is Hazardous to Your Health," *Science* 14 (January 2011) vol. 331, no. 6014: 138–40.
6. http://theforgivenessproject.com/stories/bassam-aramin-palestine/.
7. Dr. Daniel J. Siegel, *Mindsight: The New Science of Personal Transformation* (New York: Random House, 2010), 59–63.
8. Bruce Feiler, "The Stories That Bind Us," NYTimes.com, March 15, 2013, http://www.nytimes.com/2013/03/17/fashion/the-family-stories-that-bind-us-this-life.html?pagewanted=all&_r=2&.
9. Michael Lapsley with Stephen Karakashian, *Redeeming the Past: My Journey from Freedom Fighter to Healer* (Ossining, NY: Orbis Books, 2012), 162.
10. Kia Scherr is cofounder and president of One Life Alliance (onelifealliance .org), a global peace initiative that is bringing tools of peace to education, business, and government.
11. Bryan Sykes, *The Seven Daughters of Eve: The Science That Reveals Our Genetic Ancestry* (New York: W. W. Norton & Company, 2002); http://en.wikipedia.org/wiki/Mitochondrial_Eve#Further_reading.
12. Julie H. Hall and Frank D. Fincham, "Self-Forgiveness: The Stepchild of Forgiveness Research," *Journal of Social and Clinical Psychology* 24, no. 5 (2005): 621–37.
13. Brené Brown, "Four (Totally Surprising) Life Lessons We All Need to Learn," Oprah.com, http://www.oprah.com/spirit/Life-Lessons-We-All-Need-to-Learn-Brene-Brown/2.
14. Elizabeth Kübler-Ross, *Death: The Final Stage of Growth* (New York: Simon and Schuster, 1986), 96.
15. Combatants for Peace, http://cfpeace.org/?page_id=2.

Other Books by Desmond Tutu from HarperOne

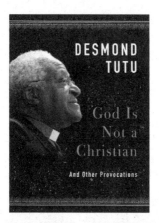

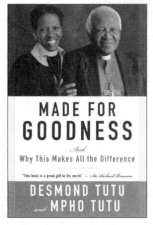

Available wherever books and e-books are sold

HarperOne
An Imprint of HarperCollins*Publishers*